# REAL-WORLD ANALYTICS

# REAL-WORLD ANALYTICS

*A business leader's concise inside view
of how to build and manage
analytical teams to drive real results
in today's Big Data Craze*

## MICHAEL KOUKOUNAS

**FCP**

*Full Court Press
Englewood Cliffs, New Jersey*

*First Edition*

Copyright © 2014 by Michael Koukounas

Published in the United States of America
by Full Court Press, 601 Palisade Avenue
Englewood Cliffs, NJ 07632
www.fullcourtpressnj.com

ISBN 978-1-938812-31-6
Library of Congress Control No. 2014936366

*Editing and Book Design by Barry Sheinkopf
for Bookshapers (www.bookshapers.com)
Cover art courtesy istockphoto.com
Colophon by Liz Sedlack*

TO MY WIFE

*who enthusiastically encouraged me*
*to write about a subject*
*she has absolutely no interest in*

## ACKNOWLEDGMENTS

To my editor and publisher Barry Sheinkopf, without whose guidance I would never have written this book. Also I want to thank all my colleagues over my career; from our successes and failures, I have learned so much. Undoubtedly, working in a world of data and analytics, any successes I have been a part of were the result of a team effort. I wish I could list you all, if for no other reason than that many of you had to put up with my slow learning curve. I suppose, these days, that is what social media are for.

# TABLE OF CONTENTS

# TABLES AND FIGURES

# CHAPTER 1

## ANALYTICS IN THE REAL WORLD

TODAY, DATA ABOUT YOU—everything from personal information about who you are, to what you are doing, to where and how you are doing it—are everywhere. From the activities and apps on your cell phone, to the web sites you surf on your laptop or tablet, to the purchases you make with credit cards, all these bits and pieces of your life are getting recorded and stored somewhere. And you're no exception to the rule: The same thing is happening to all of us.

Some of this information is recorded to help us out. For example, more and more, the devices we use every day, from our cars to our appliances, are communicating with *us*. They often tell us where we are, how efficiently they (or sometimes we) are performing, and whether a need for maintenance has suddenly arisen. Sometimes such information can be helpful—although I find the sleep app on my daughter's phone, which tracks the completeness and quality of her evening slumbers, a bit much. I don't need *my* phone to tell me that I need more sleep.

I also find it mildly annoying when my car sends me both an email *and* a text on its efficiency and maintenance needs. I suspect the car is very starved for attention when it keeps sending me text/emails warning me that I need to do something but I have chosen to ignore.

On the other hand, it's gratifying when the workout app on my phone congratulates me on completing a bike ride and tells me how well I did against other riders who have covered the same route. Who doesn't like a little encouragement after working out for a few hours, though I suspect the app is too generous—no matter how slowly I pedal, I always seem to beat some other riders and place in the top ten for at least some part of my route.

With data storage becoming cheaper and easier to acquire, more and more companies are ferreting away these seemingly endless streams of data in the hope that, somewhere in the future, they will find a way to use them to drive improved business results, or even a new revenue stream. Welcome to era of "Big Data," a misleading and overused term that I try to avoid.

All these data only becomes meaningful if someone can interpret them, segment them, analyze them, and sometimes use them to predict a useful outcome. Today, armies of analysts troll through these data streams daily, hourly, fishing for insights into an assortment of business needs.

More and more companies are building analytical teams as well, to help them interpret the data they have assembled, often combined with third-party data sets.

The problem is that building and managing analytical

teams is not easy. There is, and always has been, a large demand across the globe for analytical talent. Moreover, those talented folks—smart as they are—often don't know how to develop analytical solutions that are both efficient and implementable.

This book attempts to bridge that crucial gap. It offers the following:

Section 1: Four key elements that drive strong, impactful analytics

Section 2: How to apportion the key responsibilities in designing an analytical organization

Section 3: Six steps to developing successful analytics.

## An Example of Good Analytics that Cannot Be Used

What do stealing over 6.5 million gallons of diesel fuel, and data analytics, have in common? Actually, quite a lot. Today, data and analytics have become the front line in a lot of law enforcement work. Moreover, good analytics often help identify the best corrective action to stop fraud losses and prevent future ones.

Risk and Fraud management is one of the few occupations in the world in which you can lose millions, or tens of millions, of dollars and still keep your job. The secret is losing less than your annual budget expects you to lose. The problems for most credit or fraud managers arise when they start to lose more than they figured they would at the beginning of the year.

When my company lost over 6.5 million gallons of diesel fuel, people started losing their jobs.

Most large petroleum companies have privately labeled gas cards that help the companies create brand loyalty. Early in my career, I worked for a financial institution that provided such cards to a large oil company.

Perpetrators of credit-card fraud usually understand that financial institutions are willing to absorb a certain amount of it in order to provide a better, easier, and friend-lier customer experience. Banks could stop credit card fraud tomorrow, but in order to do so, they would make using their cards so onerous that most consumers would cut them up.

The gas-card portfolio at my bank had, on average, $300,000 in fraud losses a month. Once fraudsters identi-fied gaps in the card-authorization process, those losses es-calated to over $2,000,000 every month.

That's when my bank went into overdrive. We wanted to understand what was driving the theft of so much diesel fuel, so we hired a national private detective agency to investigate, which provided us with nice videos of how the fraudsters were getting away with it. Most of the fraud was centered in south Florida, and, one night, the detectives had the cameras rolling when a large pick-up truck pulled up to a diesel pump with an empty 750-gallon polypropylene marine gas tank tied down in the back bed. The driver and his accomplice inserted both diesel hoses from the island into the empty tank, took out a stack of counterfeit gas cards, and started to fill the tank. Every time a card reached its daily gas limit, the driver replaced it with another off the stack and continued to fill up the tank. Even with two hoses working to fill that enormous tank, it took them over two hours.

You'd assume that a truck parked at a gas island for over two hours might raise some suspicions. Where was the station attendant during all this activity? The gas attendant, a kid manning the station at night was busy, as it turned out. The detective agency filmed him being given a twenty-dollar bill by the driver of the truck to fetch some pizza. To make the scheme work, there had to have been collusion with the station.

Once the marine gas tank was full, the fraudsters called their friends to pull in behind them at the pumps before they took off, so the process could continue with a new empty marine gas tank.

The detectives followed the pick-up truck into a deserted spot in Everglades, where it came to a stop next to a 10,000-gallon eighteen-wheel tanker into which it could empty it contents.

Once the gas station ran out of diesel fuel, the 10,000-gallon tanker would roll out of the Everglades, pull up into the same station, and sell back the stolen diesel for a fraction of the wholesale cost. The next day, the gas station would submit the credit card receipts to the bank for payment. The bank, by contract, has to pay the station for diesel sold on gas cards within twenty-four hours. And then the bank was left trying to collect for gas supposedly sold to customers who never existed.

This activity took place simultaneously at dozens of gas stations across Florida and Texas.

Figuring out how the scheme worked took good detective work worthy of a *Law and Order* episode. But where do data analytics come in?

## Queue up the Geeks

Clearly a lot analytics had to be done to identify the location and scale of this fraud activity. Analytics were also needed to identify the gap in the authorization process the fraudsters were exploiting.

The real question, though, is: *How could analytics prevent these industrious fraudsters from executing their scheme in the first place?*

At the time, I was managing a team of data scientists, really smart mathematicians and statisticians. One Monday morning in the middle of the fraud attack, I came into the office to find that one my team members had spent the weekend building a fraud model to predict which of these transactions had a high probability of being fraudulent.

The modeler was an eager young guy we had hired earlier in the year. He was a smart twenty-something from a mid-West school who had just completed his master's in statistics. He had constructed a sophisticated neural net model that performed very well in identifying just that type of fraud transaction.

A good fraud model has a low false-positive rate but

captures a high percentage of fraud—at least 20 percent of the fraud at a 30-to-1 false positive rate. (False positives are transactions that the model identifies as potentially fraudulent but that, upon investigation, turn out not to be fraudulent.) Which in turn means that, in the needle-in-the-haystack process that fraud mitigation tends to be, you have to investigate 29 good transactions to stop the one fraud from happening.

This young fellow's new model captured an amazing 50 percent of the fraud at a false positive rate of 6 to 1. Unfortunately, though this was an outstanding performance, especially for a quick-and-dirty fraud model built over a weekend, we could not use this new fraud model. Here's why.

## Real-World Solutions vs. Laboratory Solutions

Good analytics in a *laboratory* need only a handful of key ingredients:

- Access to historical data that can create a sample containing the dependent variable you are trying to predict—in this case, a sample with known fraudulent and non-fraud transactions
- Historical data that can be used as independent variables, that is, data that simulate information available, at the time of your sample, of known fraudulent transactions. These data that can be used to help predict if a transaction is or is not

fraudulent.
- Access to good modeling tools
- A really good modeler who understands the tools, the data, and the domain they are trying to work in

In the diesel fraud example above, the modeler had access to the first three items listed above but revealed gaps in the fourth item on the list: domain knowledge.

He had access to a large quantity of known fraudulent transactions to train a model. He had access to a large quantity of historical data too, with a hundred or so variables that could be used as independent variables to predict fraudulent transactions. He also had access to sophisticated tools for developing fraud models.

What he did *not* understand was the domain that the model would need to be deployed in, and the business situation.

### Fraudster Fun

Two factors made the diesel fraud possible. First, the fraudsters exploited a weakness in the magnetic stripe on the back of private-label gas card. All credit cards have magnetic stripes that contain information—and, in all cases nowadays, *some* device to mitigate counterfeit fraud. In the case of cards the fraudsters were using, the magnetic strip contained an account number *and nothing else*.

The second factor was that, when the fraud occurred

in the 1990s, many gas stations had no access to today's fast modems used to access the card authorization systems— and the dial-up modems then in use were slow and cumbersome. Imagine a customer having to wait at a pump for a dial-up modem to squeak and squawk as it connected to a bank for authorizing the credit card before someone can pump gas!

The gas company wanted to make it *easy* for their customers to use their gas cards, not more difficult. This meant that, as long as the transaction contained a mathematically valid account number, the card was accepted at the pump. "Mathematically valid" meant that the card number was in the right format, *not* that it had actually been issued and associated with an open account and a known consumer.

### Reality Is Never Easy

So the model that my young modeler had created worked very well in a laboratory environment but was not, to our regret, practical in the real world.

In order for it to work, the petroleum company would have had to invest millions of dollars, and many months, in an effort to change its point-of-sale register systems to accept all these transactions and return the card-authorization system's results. Moreover (an even longer pole to erect in that tent), the company would have had to mandate all their gas stations and franchisees to invest thousands of bucks in new point-of-sales and communication equipment to authorize every transaction. Even if the company had issued this mandate, it would have taken over eighteen months to get all stations to comply and implement a robust point-of-sale systems change.

The mistake the modeler made was, in fact, the same one *many* data analysts make, especially in today's Big-Data Frenzy: *Start With The Data.* I regularly see organizations caught up in this Big Data obsession, this up-to-the-minute gold rush in which far too many people, data scientists and business managers alike, believe that there is gold in all those new and growing piles of data— and that, if only they can crack the code with the right statistical tool and some ingenuity, they will discover millions of dollars of value.

Please don't take my reservations over this data craze as a vote against data and analytics. Quite the opposite: I have built a career on *using* data and analytics to drive multi-million-dollar impacts, so I am a true believer in data analytics. But I have learned that data and analytics only drive business impacts if they are executed with an understanding of how they are going to be *implemented.*

What my young modeler did not understand was the *domain*—the business issues surrounding this fraud attack. This is, in fact, where *most* data analytics fail. Starting with a pile of data and panning for gold usually doesn't work, and I have seen really good analytics fall flat for the very same reason: a failure to understand how the real world works and how these analytics will be implemented to drive business impacts.

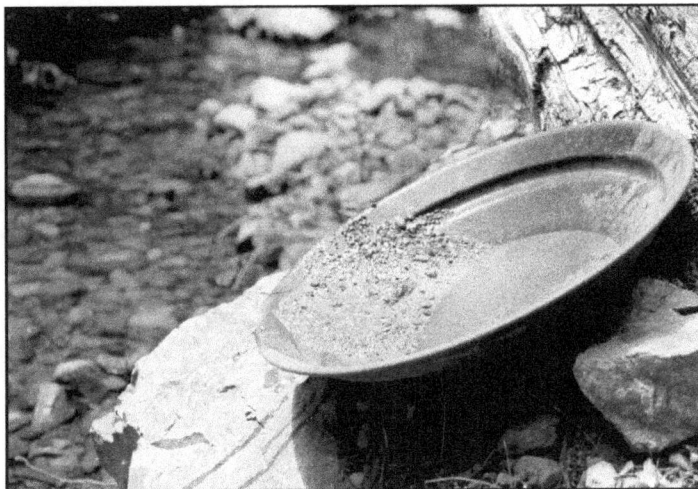

This book considers how to develop analytics that will work within a domain you are trying to impact. I want to examine issues you need to consider *before* you start pulling up all that data: how the analytics will influence the decision makers, what concerns need to be evaluated, and the most practical way to get the results you're looking for.

These issues include the following:

- Are the data problematic from a reputational, legal, cost, or implementation perspective?
- Where are the critical touch points, and how does this analytic impact those touch points?
- What actions is the analytic recommending, and how does that drive business impacts?

# CHAPTER 2

## WHAT'S "ANALYTICS"?

RECENTLY THERE HAS BEEN a lot in the news about the government spying on individuals' email and Internet activities. I am surprised people are shocked by these activities. Access to information about everyone has been available in different formats for years. I have done business with a private company that had access to the sites people surfed on the Internet and the material they were looking at. While that company was non-profit and the information was being gathered to catch child predators, it nevertheless meant that Internet providers were providing your data to third parties—exactly what we're now complaining about.

From movies, to last weekend's sports tickets, to the *latte* you buy with your phone, from restaurant reservations to doctor's appointments, more and more is done online and recorded in multiple places.

In the past, business analyses occurred when someone was persistent enough to lay their hands on some data, usually somewhat old, and they often used it to manually create graphs. With some luck, and perhaps intuition, these people might identify some trend, or be struck by some insight, in those graphs. The process was tedious, because gathering the data was onerous and very labor intensive. Also, the person doing the analysis needed to have enough domain expertise to understand what they were looking at and what a "trend"*meant*.

When computers became widely available, storage of data became easier, but even then the data were not always easy to get to, and few systems applications were developed with the idea of *allowing* for easy access to data for analysis.

For example, AT&T stored everyone's phone bill for many years, which is a lot of data. Phone bill data were stored as an exact image of a customer's monthly bill, as if someone had taken an electronic snapshot of the bill and stored it.

The problem with this approach to data storage was that, while the imaged billing data was very useful for customer inquiries at a call center, it couldn't be used to figure out who your best customers were. To complicate matters further, each Baby Bell used a different bill format, so a bill from Bell South was different from a bill from NYNEX. Therefore, if the AT&T Marketing team wanted to understand who their best customers were and what they might look like, they couldn't extract answers from the data—which were enormous, very timely, and very complete. But, in their presentation, they were also too uneven and too cumbersome to use for analytical purposes or to create business opportunities.

## Data Are the Table Stakes

So, in the past, data were not always easy to get to and were therefore *precious*, and the definition of "analytics," or the practice of discovering meaning in data, necessarily included the *gathering*, as well as the evaluation, of that data.

Today, by contrast, data are *everywhere* and occur in all sorts of forms. Usually, however, they fall into two categories:

- Historical, meaning the data reflect events in the past
- Real-time, meaning the data reflect what is going on now

Now that data *are* everywhere, how does that change the definition of analytics?

At an IBM Big Data conference, I once had a conversation with one of the senior IBM managers and asked her about how she saw the role of data in analytics evolving. Her answer was very straightforward: "Data are the table's stakes in today's world of analytics."

Google "business analytics definition," and you will get over 15 million hits. Go to YouTube and search "business analytics, "and you can watch videos of over 1.5 million experts explaining, all in very confident tones, many with excellent graphics, what business analytics are to various audiences. Clearly, there is no end to the number of experts explaining what "business analytics" are, and you may find even the challenge of grasping the underlying idea daunting.

While analytics, and the math supporting them, can indeed be very complex, however, I have taught my share classes on analytics, and I find it helpful to make the definition of "analytics" simple, as revealed in the following syllogism:

Business analytics use data to make better decisions.

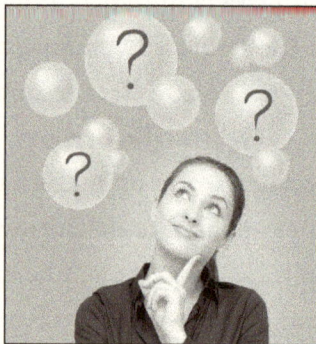

Who makes decisions?  People make decisions.

So business analytics are about people evaluating data to make better decisions.

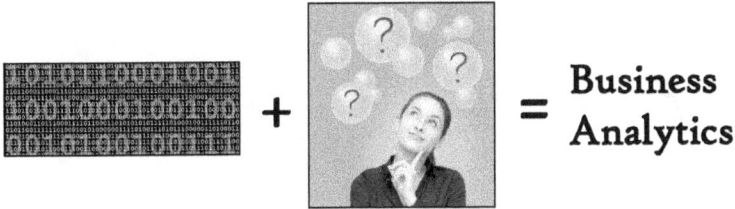 **Business Analytics**

### People

Businesses engage in this analytical exercise in a variety of ways:

- CEOs make strategic decisions about whether to bring products to market.
- Risk Managers decide which loans to accept.
- Marketing teams decide which offers to present, and to which customers.
- Consumers decide which offers to accept.

All of these decisions can be made more efficient with analytics.

# SECTION 1

# FOUR KEY ELEMENTS THAT CREATE MEANINGFUL ANALYTICS

# CHAPTER 3

## THE ATOM METHOD
## OF DEVELOPING
## ANALYTICS CAPABILITIES

I HAVE COME ACROSS very smart and accomplished business leaders who preserve the perspective that analytical teams consist of a few good geeks and some data. These business leaders don't understand how analytics teams that develop strong, sustainable analytical solutions really are more complex than that, and need investment. Usually it takes two changes for most business leaders to learn that lesson. The first change is that business leaders find a large portion of their revenue is tied directly or indirectly to the output of the analytics team. The second is that bad analytics, or no analytics, result in the loss of a large part of their revenue.

Only when poor analytics result in significant revenue loss do these business leaders try to determine why the analytics failed and what needs to happen to mitigate future failures. The next section considers the four key elements that will help to avoid the success–failure business cycle and create an analytical team that will generate sustainable quality analytics.

## *The Issues with Part-Time Analytics: Let Me in, Coach, I'm Ready to Play Today*

In most organizations there is some ambitious person all revved up and ready to unleash their inner Geek. Typically, these enthusiastic part-time analysts lay their hands on some data and, in their slow periods or off time, decide they are going to impress their management by conducting some analytics. They frequently create a report, and possibly some graphs, that they offer in a presentation that includes some previously unknown insights about the business. Some of the more ambitious part-time analysts perhaps learn as well how to use some modeling software to predict an outcome or optimize a business process.

Assuming these insights have a large enough business impact, management may be impressed enough to decide to act on these analytical findings.

And this is often where the problems begin.

Moving from an analytical environment, frequently on someone's PC or data server, to a production environment that drives business impacts requires a level of detail and effort that most of these part-time analytics cannot support. They run into a variety of problems including:

- Data-definition issues
- Sustainability issues
- Implementation issues

Let's quickly explore each of these potential problems.

## Data-Definition Issues

Data definitions from part-time analytics often differ from other reporting or productions variables. Frequently, somewhere along the way, someone in the organization will determine that they cannot reconcile some part of the part-time analytic with another, more established, means of analytic reporting. This difference is often due to data-definition inconsistency between the two analytics, even if they are using the same sources of data. Unfortunately, differences between the part-time analytic and the more established reporting will often call into question the validity of the part-time analytic. In this way, the part-time analyst will suddenly have to put in a lot of time reconciling, defending, or redeveloping their work.

## Sustainability Issues

*All analytics have a self-life*—some faster than others—but this is a fact. Therefore, someone has to maintain these analytics, and part-time analysts do not often have enough time, or the infrastructure, to do their day jobs and maintain their new analytics.

Also, to maintain any analytics requires that they be well documented. Part-time analytics are often *not* well documented; moreover, rarely is any documentation updated as changes take place, and changes happen often. So when the individual who created these part-time analytics moves on to a new department or leaves the company, there's usually no one who can answer questions about the analytic's current performance. Since no one can, it often gets thrown away, or the company has to spend money redeveloping it.

### *Implementation Issues*

As we saw in the gas-card example, moving analytics from an analytical environment to a production environment poses many challenges unless the analyst has taken

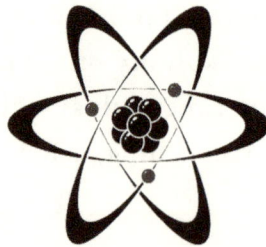

the operational environment into account when they developed their analytics.

### *The Four Key Elements in a Successful Analytic— The ATOM Method*

Rarely do successful analytics just happen. To create meaningful, actionable, and sustainable ones takes deliberate planning and investment. Four key elements, or building blocks, are required in order to develop analytical capacity that can construct and maintain successful analytics.

I call these four elements the "**ATOM**" system of developing analytical capacity.

**A***ccess to Data:* Painless and quick access to data (including internal and third-party) that are relevant and actionable.

**T***alent:* Analytical talent that can evaluate the data quickly and generate impactful insights.

**O***perational Knowledge:* Understanding the business environment that is being impacted, so that a solution can be implemented quickly.

**M***aintenance:* All analytics need to be maintained and updated based on performance feedback.

Early in my career, I quickly learned how expensive errors become when an analytical organization doesn't possess these four key elements.

At one company, I was put in charge of the analytical teams; one of the changes I soon made was to place a senior analyst in charge of reviewing inquiries coming from customers about their credit applications. In the past, a non-analytical person would have managed this type of inquiry. As the senior analyst investigated these customer inquiries, they identified a series of errors in the credit application system.

For example, the analyst discovered that, for some customers, the more delinquent a customer had been in the past on other credit products, the *better* the credit score they received. Obviously, customers with poor credit history should not be getting higher credit scores than customers with a pristine credit history.

What we later discovered was that the analysts who developed this application solution had:

- managed both the development of the analytical solution and the implementation of the solution into the application process
- developed their own suite of data attributes for this new solution instead of using the existing attributes
- because of a lack of business knowledge, built this application process by replicating an older credit process that did not apply to the types of decisions the new process needed to make

To no one's surprise, the analyst who developed the application process had left the company over three years before, and no one knew where any of his documentation was or whether there had ever been any.

We also discovered that this process had been in place for several years with no one responsible for maintaining it. When I asked why, I received the following explanations:

- Resources were lacking
- Other priorities always took precedence
- Access to data to complete the maintenance work

was onerous and time consuming

- Documentation was lacking
- (After several questions, and sheepishly), no one was interested in doing maintenance work

The problem was that, for years, these errors in the application process had gone undetected and, as a result, had under certain conditions approved or declined credit for the wrong customers. It was later determined that these errors caused millions of dollars in lost revenue (customers declined who should have been approved) and incremental credit losses (customers approved who should have been declined).

In addition to the financial losses, the errors also created both regulatory and reputation issues for the institution. Fixing these errors would impact many customers and required a lot of time and money to remediate.

As the team looked to do so, the absence of documentation presented a big hurdle. No one understood how to safely repair these errors. Without the documentation, the team could easily have repaired one problem but unknowingly create two new ones in the process. Therefore, the only practical option was to redevelop the entire application—a very expensive, resources-intensive, time-consuming process. Having the four key elements for analytics in place would have prevented these costly errors.

In the subsequent chapters of Section 1, I will review each of the four elements in the ATOM system, including issues, some solutions, and consequences a manager of analytical talents needs to address.

# CHAPTER 4

## ACCESS TO DATA

MANY BUSINESSES BELIEVE THAT, because they are storing enormous amounts of data about the products they sell, their customers, or their many business processes, access to that data is not an issue. However, merely storing data does not mean that access to those data, or to the format the data are stored in, allows for *efficient* analytics.

Barriers exist to accessing data, which create friction in the analytical process. These include:

- Data stored across various systems
- Data stored in various formats
- Data definitions not being maintained
- Absence of an easy way to consolidate the data
- No efficient method of accessing the data

Often in companies, data are stored in various systems across different business functions and different business units. Product *order* data are, for example, often stored in a different system from product *manufacturing* or product *performance* data. Consequently, for the analyst, access to data often involves retrieving it from multiple systems environments.

In addition, because the data are stored in different systems and various parts of the business, they often have different access capabilities, stored cycles, and storage capacities. Some systems may store many years of data with significant detail about each activity, while others only store a summary of yesterday's activities.

Finally, as analysts wade through these different systems and data storage complexities, they will frequently find that the data elements are not well defined, or that similar data attributes are not formatted consistently, or that the definitions may not be well maintained over time. Without a thorough understanding of the data stored in these systems, an analyst pulling data together for an analytic has to navigate a minefield of data completeness, timing, and accuracy issues. Without a strong understanding of the data being used, the analyst can easily end up with flawed conclusions.

As a consequence, analytical leaders need to find an efficient way to manage the data needs of their analytical talent.

Two solutions to this challenge that work well together in creating a more seamless process of accessing data for analytics are:

- Building a data management team to support the analytics teams

• Creating an analytical environment that supports your business needs

## Data Management Team

If an organization really desires to be in the business of analyzing data, creating a team to administer them is an excellent idea. Data management teams support the analysts by running the *Extract, Transform, and Load* (ETL) process. Here are a few good reasons why data management teams are a good investment:

• They maintain efficient access to data from various sources
• They provide better maintenance of data definitions
• They offer more efficient use of analyst time

Let's explore each of these reasons for a data management team in greater detail.

## Accessing Data from Various Systems

One of the responsibilities of the data management team is to identify new sources of data and to then make those data accessible. For both internal and external sources of data, the Data Management Team can investigate how complete a new source of data is, define the data elements that are available, and determine how to best store and make those data accessible to the business.

Furthermore, the data management team ensures that existing data sources are available to both the analysts (to develop solutions) and the production systems (to implement the solutions). For example, at one company I worked for, the Data Management Team processed more than 300 million customer accounts each evening and loaded the results into a variety of production systems every morning. In this way, the company had access each day to the most up-to-date information about its customers. Without the data management team, this process would never have been implemented.

### Better Maintenance of Data Definitions

One essential ingredient in analytics is that your analytical teams have access to have an updated and validate *data dictionary*, a document that defines the data attributes in your data files, including any calculations, or adjustments made, to these attributes.

So one very important aspect of data quality is maintaining and validating the *definitions* of the data attributes— a continuous responsibility as the data definitions evolve over time. In addition to helping to support the process of storing and retrieving data for the analyst, the data management team's responsibilities include managing the *quality* of the data as the data definitions evolve over time.

Data evolve in this way for a number of reasons, including changes in the organizations systems, products, customer habits, competition, and regulatory changes, all of which will force a shift in those definitions moving forward. It's important that individuals are in place who work to ensure that, as the data go through this evolution, the organization understands and documents the changes. Having a team of professionals manage the data environment ensures that the analysts have access to data that are well defined, and that any issues of completeness, timeliness, and accuracy are fully understood. Furthermore, for data being used in a solution, the data management team works with the system teams to ensure that the data elements are defined correctly.

Without a full understanding of the data being used in an analytic, the analyst can easily draw the wrong conclusions. Moreover, without someone working with the system implementation teams to ensure the right data definitions are being applied in the production solutions, the results of the analytic can easily be adversely affected.

I have observed analytical teams who take on these ETL responsibilities—frequently out of necessity rather than by design. Strong analytical talent prefers to be analyzing data instead of maintaining or working hard to make those data accessible. Yet, regularly, analysts end up supporting the ETL steps—not because they want to, but because they have to.

Unfortunately, the data maintenance step is an ongoing, full-time job that is best left to professionals who are trained to manage and manipulate data. Making analysts support the ETL process results in short-changing both the analytics and ETL processes.

In addition, being a smart analyst doesn't mean you are good at managing data. When analysts are obliged to support the ETL process, a proliferation of data attributes results.

For example, at one of the banks I worked at, there were over a hundred different definitions of a customer's 90-day delinquency profile. Now, most people would believe that customers had only one version of their payment history, which would show when in the past, and for how much, a customer went 90 days delinquent. Moreover, most of these hundred-plus versions of a customer's 90-day delinquency profile resulted in slightly different answers. If analysts misunderstood the definition of the version they were using, they could easily draw the wrong conclusion from their results.

Many of the organizations I have worked with are managing thousands of often-redundant data attributes created by the analysts. The proliferation of data attributes has become a resources drain and a barrier for efficient implementation.

## *More Efficient Use of Analyst Time*

Having a professional data management team means that your data definitions are more efficiently maintained and data access is more economical. This makes it easier for the analyst to access data and quickly understand what data they are looking at. Data management teams allow analysts to spend more of their time finding new business insights instead of accessing and managing data.

Furthermore, analytical talent is expensive and hard to retain, so keeping those analysts focused on what they are good at, finding business insights, usually results in better solutions and happier analysts.

## Analytics Environments

Analytical environments are computer systems where data are stored, and easily accessed and manipulated by analysts as they search for insights or trends.

Today, a variety of platforms and software allows for vast amounts of data to be accessed and manipulated with incredible speed and efficiency. There are companies of all shapes and sizes trying to sell these platforms and software tools to businesses that have analytical needs. This book is not going to cover the pros and cons of the various systems or software packages available. I *will* address some questions about how to *approach* developing an analytical environment.

Many companies start by creating server space where they can store the data, analytical software for manipulating the data, and space to perform the analytics. As the data grow larger and the analytics more complex, the companies' space and system needs grow. Moreover, as the data grow, the software required to analyze them needs more and more complex systems to support the analysts. Many companies struggle to keep up with their analytical platform needs as these systems become larger, more complex, and more expensive to manage. Often, over time, analytics that would normally now take days, as they need to be staged in order to find the space needed to process.

These days, many companies are investing, or considering investing, large sums of money in larger and faster analytical systems. These companies need to understand all their options before making a large investment in a new system platform.

My concern with building these high-speed platforms for analytics has nothing to do with the technology. It is centered on the expertise of the organization that will be *building and maintaining* these platforms. Let me say again: As companies add analytical staff and larger and more complex datasets, their need for larger and more power analytical platforms grows. How many organizations really have the expertise and the ability to fully understand analytic systems needs? Moreover, how many of these companies have the expertise to build and manage platforms that can easily *expand* as the analytical needs grow?

Managing data platforms is often the responsibility of the Chief Technology Office. But these are companies with expertise in selling cell phones, marketing apparel, or insurance, or in issuing credit. Often they are *not* experts in managing data and data platforms. Most would probably not be considered trusted stewards of data either.

How many times in the recent past have we heard about data breaches at some large retailer?

There *are* a number of companies around that *focus* on building and managing high-speed platforms for data storage and analytics. These companies understand what it takes to maintain such platforms, and the security needs of the data they house. They are often in a better position than a department store, financial institution, or telephone company to manage high-speed analytical environments.

For example, I once partnered with a small company that conducted merchandising analytics for many national retailers. The company supported retailers with analytics that helped them optimize pricing and promotions, with merchandise planning and forecasting, and with their inventory management.

The company took in vast quantities of data daily from its clients, including data about the products being sold at hundreds of locations, their inventory, web-based activities, even data about the weather. The company created very powerful and sophisticated analytical tools that updated continuously as new data were received. These tools allowed the executives at the retailer's headquarters, as well as store managers, to make informed decisions about what products to stock, where to stock them, and at what price.

When I met the company CEO, I was surprised by how they were executing all these analytics. Their data storage and processing was not done on in-house computers, as I would have expected, but on the Cloud. These

Cloud environments are managed by companies that focus on renting out space on enormous high-speed data platforms.

My first question was about data security. The CEO quickly explained that the Cloud companies made their living out of data security, whereas his company made its out of analyzing data. Renting analytical and data space, he explained, significantly reduced the complexity of his company infrastructure. This allowed his staff to focus on the process of actually analyzing data. He also told me that his company stripped the personal information off all the data it got from its clients, thereby making those data even more secure.

The CEO informed me in addition that, by renting data and analytical space instead of building a large in-house data system, his company only paid for the analytical space the company needed instead of having to build systems in *anticipation* of growth. Therefore, as clients and data needs changed, he could quickly contract or expand his company's analytical system needs.

Undoubtedly there are times when building in-house analytics and data system is the right choice; I'm merely advocating an exploration of the benefits of using third-party systems *before* making the investment in a large in-house platform.

# CHAPTER 5

## TALENT

A S THE WORLD PILES up more data, and more industries and companies turn to those data for a competitive edge, the demand for analytical talent continues to grow everywhere. As it does, attracting and retaining strong analytical talent becomes a big challenge.

To meet this ever-increasing demand, many companies have already open up vast analytical offices in countries around the globe—in Eastern Europe, Latin America, India, and the Far East. Anywhere there are reserves of students with quantitative skills, companies are hiring up analytical talent.

An analytical leader needs to be focused on a few key problems when hiring and managing talent (see Table 1).

### Table 1: Talent Issues

| |
|---|
| Attrition is inevitable but manageable if planned for. |
| Analytics is an innate talent, so managers need to develop processes to screen for talented analysts. |

| |
|---|
| Domain expertise is expensive but necessary; therefore, experts need to be leveraged efficiently. |
| Analytical team size matters. |

In this chapter, I want to introduce you to these issues and identify the consequences that a manger of analytical talent needs to address. *Real-World Analytics* will cover most of the techniques for mitigating these issues in *Section 2: Designing Analytical Organizations.*

## Attrition

With the demand for analytical talent so high, it is inevitable that all analytical shops will have some turnover.

In analytical offices all over the world, I have observed natural points of attrition in the career cycle of the talent. For example in the second to third year out of school, many analysts leave the company they are currently with as they have gained enough experience to get a sizable *raise* (20%–30%) from a new company. In Years 5–7, analysts will often move to a new company in an effort to gain more *managerial* experience. And in Years 10–12, stronger analysts with domain knowledge and communication skills will move in search of *executive* managerial roles.

*As a consequence,* analytical teams need to develop a strong pipeline of talent to ensure the work is not disrupted as the current talent inevitably turns over. (See *Chapter 10: Build for Continuity,* for ways to manage attrition.)

## Analytics Is an Innate Talent

Analysts are individuals who possess and enjoy an instinctive ability to organize data to solve business problems. They get pleasure from the challenge of taking seemingly meaningless data and finding trends in them that can drive results.

In many years of managing analytical teams, I have observed that you can often train analytical talent how to efficiently conduct analytics, but *only* as long as they possess the instinct for finding insights in the data. Individuals who do not *possess* this innate ability are usually not very good analysts.

So, as organizations staff up junior analytical talent, they need a process that quickly identifies which analysts possess that innate ability for finding insights, and which do not. (See *Chapter 10: Build for Continuity*, for ways to develop an efficient pipeline of talent.)

## Domain Expertise

A good rule of thumb for analytical talent is: The more domain expertise an analyst has, the more expensive that talent will be. Also, the more obscure or in demand their domain expertise, the more expensive it will be.

Hiring and staffing analytical teams is a challenge, but staffing analytical roles that require specific industry experience and skills becomes a real challenge and is often expensive.

Here's an example. I have more than once had to fill management roles on small business analytics teams.

These are usually a combination of analytics skills, management experience, and knowledge about how to use various sources of small-business data to lend money or market to small business entrepreneurs. Finding the right combination of these skills and experiences is never easy. Often candidates have the analytical skills and management experience but *haven't* worked with small businesses. Or they have the small-business experiences but not the analytical or management skills. As a result, when I *do* find good candidates, they know their value and are often highly paid. So I've had to offer a salary as large as mine, though their responsibilities were a lot smaller.

*As a result*, analytical teams need to think about how to organize in a way that leverages critical domain expertise efficiently and create a mechanism for training junior talent and passing on critical knowledge. (See *Chapters 10* and *11* for ways to efficiently leverage experts.)

## Size Matters

As the demand for analytical talent continues to grow, smaller analytical shops are going to find it difficult to retain their most experience people. Experienced analytical talents often gravitate to larger analytical organizations, where they will have more career opportunities and more opportunities to learn marketable skills.

Also, analytical organizations that have limitations in the data to which they have access, or the types of solutions the analytical teams develop solutions for, will have a tougher time attracting and retaining talent. Experienced analytical talent is often attracted by the opportunity to work with different types of data and on different types of solutions that create marketable skills for them.

*Therefore*, analytical leaders need to find ways to consolidate talent and provide the analyst the opportunity to work on a variety of projects as junior analysts build their skills sets. (See *Chapter 12: Size of an Analytical Team.*)

## Consolidate Analytical Talent

One option available to analytical leaders in mitigating the size issue is to consolidate disparate analytical teams buried inside various business units and functions. Many companies have individual analysts, or small groups of analysts, buried in just this way. By consolidating these teams into one group, the organization will create more career opportunities for the staff.

Consolidation will also allow for best-practices sharing, and for the staff to get to work on different solutions across the company instead of just the little corner of the company each of them came from.

Consolidation also creates opportunities for more experienced analysts to help train less-experienced ones. Consolidation creates larger team as well, which can help attract experienced talent.

In these ways, consolidation can help create a better work environment, mitigate attrition risk, and make recruiting new talent easier. In addition to consolidation, *Chapter*

*12: Size of the Analytical Team* discusses tools that can help determine the size of the team the organization requires.

While I am believer in consolidating analytical talent, I have to mention that many managers of analytical teams don't. They will argue that consolidating creates bureaucracy, which leads to inefficiency and loss of creativity. These proponents of decentralized analytics will point to small analytical companies that are successful niche players and compete effectively against much larger shops.

I would not argue that such small shops *can* be successful; I haveseen many that *have* been successful. But as businesses evolve, becoming more dependent on analytics, analytical solutions become more difficult to maintain, and the need for talent grows, consolidation of talent is a strong tool .

# CHAPTER 6

## OPERATIONAL KNOWLEDGE

I WAS RECENTLY INVITED to a conference at which I attended a dinner with more than twenty senior analytical executives from various organizations. We were seated around a rather large table—all of us with twenty years of experience, or more, managing analytical teams.

As the wine flowed, and conversation turned from weather, family, and vacations to business—and the topic that generated the most enthusiastic engagement was the discussion on talent.

That the talent issue was discussed for over an hour, I did not find unusual. What surprised me was that we weren't talking about how to hold onto talented analysts (though that's always a challenge), but about their team members' ability to look at data and understand how to use them to *solve business problems.*

The executive who initiated this conversation was very passionate about the topic and added that it was one of his biggest management issues. "I can hire the smartest analysts, with Ph.D.'s in math," he said, "with statistics degrees from some of the best universities in the world, yet they often don't understand how to use data to drive a business impact." Everyone around the table agreed and offered their own examples.

They also agreed that this gap in know-how is not a result of lack of intelligence or ability on the part of these analysts. Far from it—most analysts are smart and very driven individuals. The issue wasn't their ability to execute the math, but the fact that they didn't understand the operational environment and business domain that they were trying to use analytics to help.

My diesel-fraud story is a good example of this phenomenon. The analyst built one of the best fraud models I have ever seen, from a statistical performance perspective—but one that was completely unusable from a business perspective.

## All Geeks Are Not Fungible

Executives in the C-suite often believe that, as long as they have a staff of smart analysts with master's or Ph.D.'s in math or statistics, these resources are fungible: Throw any data at them, and they will be able to manipulate them and solve almost any problem. This is a fundamental mistake many analytical teams suffer through and fail to solve for.

Additionally, the consequence of not *addressing* the issue—that is, of not having the *right* experts—is usually a lot of rework, lost sales, or poorly performing solutions. The lack of operational and domain expertise shows up in two areas of the analytic process:

- Analytical Design: When setting up an analytical design that will solve the business issue defined
- Insights: When interpreting the results of an analytic to identify insights that will drive business impacts

Business executives use two methods to resolve the problem of lack of operational knowledge.

## Single Thread

One solution many analytical teams employ to help mitigate the operational knowledge gap is *single threading their analytics through a domain expert*. The problem with this approach is that, often enough, the *only* domain expert is the executive managing the analytical team. Concerns with single-threading solutions are:

- Single-threading analytics through one person slows down the analytical process
- Single threading often limits new ideas
- Single threading can be a burden on the executive managing the team. Single-threading often drags them too deep into the details of an analytic. Moreover, the practice doesn't give these

executives time to consider other business issues.
- The single-thread solution leaves the organization
vulnerable to a single point of failure: If that
expert leaves, your productivity will fall
quickly.

That evening around the dinner table, the single-thread
method was the solution most frequently adopted by the
analytical executives, often with them themselves becoming the operational expert on their team.

## Staff Up

A second method for resolving the issue of lack of domain expertise is to go out and hire analytical talent *with*
operational expertise. The problem with this approach is
simple. . .it's very, very expensive to fill an analytical team
with experts.

Finding, hiring, and retaining analytical talent is hard
enough; hiring analytical talent with operational expertise
is usually very tough. As I mentioned in the section on
talent, the rule of thumb for analytical talent is: The more
expertise they have, the more expensive the talent—and
the more obscure or in demand their expertise, the more
expensive it will be.

*As a consequence,* analytical leaders need to find a balance between the single-thread method and loading up the
team with expensive and hard-to-find operation and do-

main experts.

How in fact to *balance* single-threading and staffing up operational and domain experts depends on the type of analytical organization the business needs, which will be discussed in *Chapter 11: Which Expertise*, and *Chapters 13–16: Types of Analytics Resources Functions Required.*

# CHAPTER 7

## MAINTENANCE

MAINTENANCE IS THE PART of analytics that is most often neglected but that is *absolutely required*. All analytics fatigue over time, and for this reason maintenance is a necessity.

Analytics solutions fatigue for a number of reasons:

- The data often change
- Products and services change
- The economy changes
- Your customer mix changes
- Your competition reacts and changes its offerings
- Laws and regulations change
- Technology is constantly evolving
- Product performance changes over time
- Consumer preferences change

Therefore, if an organization is leveraging analytical solutions to make business decisions, it faces an absolute need to monitor the performance of the analytics in order to adjust for these changes.

Often in the rush to get to the benefits associated with an analytical solution, the steps needed to ensure the analytics can be easily maintained often get ignored. Organizations that understand all analytics *require* maintenance build the resources and steps to support maintenance into their original business case supporting the analytics.

## Who Should Maintain the Analytics?

Depending on the type of analytics that are being developed, it often makes sense that the team monitoring the performance of these analytics is different from the team building them. I have often seen that analysts put so much time and effort into their work they can lose their objectivity. Having someone take a fresh look at an analyst's solution is often a good idea.

For some analytical solutions, this arm's-length oversight is a regulatory requirement. For other solutions, which were the result of a bad analytic, are very expensive, or can result in a safety issue, arm's-length oversight is *also* a very good idea. When companies invest in maintenance, moreover, they are investing in their analytical solutions to ensure they are less vulnerable to their competitors.

One of the biggest benefits of investing in maintaining analytical solutions, instead of waiting for those solutions to fatigue and fail over time, is that small maintenance updates to analytical solutions are far less onerous and expensive to implement than when solutions need to be completely replaced.

For example, when I became responsible for the analytical teams at one of the banking intuitions I worked for, the teams had just gone through a regulatory review. The regulators had determined that many of the statistical tools the bank was using had not been properly maintained, and that a number had fatigued and required replacement. One of them was a probability-of-bankruptcy model that predicted the likelihood that a customer, or potential customer, would file for bankruptcy in the next twelve months.

More than two dozen different credit products were using this bankruptcy model across various points in the customer life cycle, including:

- The application process
- The process of making offers to existing customers
- The management of existing accounts and their lines of credit
- The collections process

Replacing this bankruptcy model meant that, in addition to developing and implementing the replacement across multiple platforms, the analytical teams needed to:

- Conduct 96 different analytics to determine how to optimize the use of the new model in the decisions being made. These changes are called *policy changes* (24 products x 4 different places in the customer life cycle, using the bankruptcy model).

- Then have the proposed policy changes needed to go through the process of getting senior policy, legal, and compliance approval before the bank could implement the changes in the production systems.

- Once approved, implementing these 96 different policy changes meant inserting them into systems that used the new bankruptcy model to make customer decisions, such as approving or declining applications for credit. Therefore the analytical teams had to create 96 different system-specification documents explaining to the Technology teams what changes were required.

- In addition, once the Technology teams coded the 96 changes, but prior to implementation, the analytical teams had to user-test all 96 system changes to make sure they met their specifications.

- Post-implementation in the production system, 96 new policies changes needed to be closely monitored to make sure they were working as designed.

The aggravating part of the process was that most of that onerous and time-consuming work could have been avoided had the bank invested a *fraction* of these resources in *maintaining* the bankruptcy model and periodically *ad-*

*justing* it to meet the original performance specifications.

As *a consequence*, managers of analytical teams need to develop a process to ensure their inventory of analytics solutions is being validated and maintained over time. *Chapters 13–16: Types of Analytics Resources Functions Required* will review the maintenance process.

# DESIGNING ANALYTICAL ORGANIZATIONS

# CHAPTER 8

## ANALYTICAL ORGANIZATIONS
## COME IN ALL SHAPES AND SIZES

FIRMLY BELIEVE IN the old adage that there is no perfect organizational design. Each has its positive and negative features. Moreover, as business and customer needs evolve, so will analytical needs—and, therefore, the structure that best enables those needs will also require change.

Over my career, I have had the opportunities to work with, and evaluate, over a hundred different companies with analytical capabilities. The opportunity to assess these organizations has been the result of due-diligence activities for potential acquisitions, partnerships, or, often, working closely with customers who have their own internal analytics capabilities. These relationships have given me an opportunity to examination a number of analytical structures.

One observation I have made is that all of them have a common set of obstacles. These obstacles include the following (see Table 2):

## *Table 2: Common Obstacles in Analytical Organizations*

| |
| --- |
| Trade-off between efficiency and creativity |
| Organizing to ensure continuity |
| The great debate, "Which expertise?" |
| Team Size |
| Category of analytics resources required |

Let's explore each of these obstacles to get a better idea of what they are and how they influence an organization.

# CHAPTER 9

## TRADE-OFFS BETWEEN
## EFFICIENCY AND CREATIVITY

SOME ANALYTICAL STRUCTURES ARE well thought out; others evolve over time with little consideration for efficiency.

Recently, I came across a small analytics company that had developed a notable organizational structure. The CEO, who was working on her fourth start-up, decided to design an analytical company that maximized efficiency. She had one goal in mind: to leverage the smallest number of analytical resources possible to create and implement hundreds of analytical solutions within days or weeks. In order to facilitate this level of efficiency, she focused the structure of her company around the systems environment. I call this an extreme example of a *system-centric* analytics organization.

At this company, once the data were loaded and catalogued, the analytics environment was structured to facilitate the rapid development and deployment of solutions into production. This company employed only three full-time analysts, yet they deployed an astonishing 200+ analytical solutions annually.

The trade-off for this rapid deployment was that the analytical environment was structured with very limited flexibility. First, narrow limits were placed on how, when, and where the data could be used. In addition, this highly restricted system only leveraged one statistical technique, Logistic Regression. Now, there is nothing wrong with Logistic Regression—it's a fine analytical technique. Yet as any statistician can tell you, no one analytical technique works well for all types of data or analytical problems.

This company developed an incredibly efficient analytical environment by creating an assembly-line approach to analytics that limited the ability of the analysts to wander beyond a highly prescribed process. The trade-off the CEO was willing to accept were those very limits on the ways the analytics could be conducted, and the types of problems the company would solve.

She believed that her company's analytical environment could answer eighty to ninety percent of the types of problems its customers had. Therefore the company did not need to invest in a more flexible system. She believed greater analytical flexibility would only slow down the process of developing solutions by introducing increased complexity in how solutions are developed, that analytical complexity creates more difficulties in the implementation process, and that all this flexibility would require her to hire and retain more expensive analytical talent. From the CEO's perspective, analytical flexibility only increased her costs and reduced her margins.

Analytical organization structures frequently struggle in just this way with the trade-off between efficiency (what I call the *assembly-line* approach to analytics) and the R&D, which is a more *iterative* approach to analytics.

In the above example, the company chose to organize around simplicity and speed of delivery; other companies need analytical flexibility as they focus on the research and development of new ideas. These companies need to evaluate new sources of data or the continuous development of new products; therefore, the assembly-line approach will not work for them.

R&D, or iterative analytics, takes more time, given that these analytics need the freedom and flexibility to explore different sources of data, and different statistical techniques, in order to determine the best way to develop a solution. Many analysts *enjoy* the freedom and analytical challenge of the R&D approach to analytics.

One drawback with R&D analytics is that they usually take many months, several times longer than an assembly-line analytic. Another is that this approach often requires a lot of support resources. Because these teams work with new sources of data, unfamiliar systems, or new problems, a *number* of teams need to be involved as they evaluate options and eliminate possible but inadequate solutions.

I have repeatedly watched teams focus too much time on R&D analytics and not enough on developing practical solutions for their customers. Because R&D teams *are* inclined to be expensive, since they consume more resources and time, they need to be supervised to ensure they are focusing their efforts on appropriate long-term and big-return opportunities.

When trying to choose between an analytical structure that is more inclined to operate as an assembly line or to take an R&D approach, the decision regularly depends on the types of customer analytics the team is being asked to support.

### When to Focus on Assembly-Line Analytics

If the customer requires solutions that, for the most part, *exist today but need to be customized* to meet their current business conditions, then a focus on assembly-line analytics, built for efficiency, makes sense.

### When to Focus on R&D Analytics

If the business problems the customers are searching for solutions to require *new* analytical techniques, employ *new* sources of data, or are being implemented into processes that are *unfamiliar*, then an analytical organization focused to support R&D activities makes sense.

### When to Focus on Both

It's also not uncommon to need a combination of both R&D *and* assembly-line analytics. Frequently, analytical solutions developed through the R&D process eventually migrate over to an assembly-line process as they are customized to meet customers' changing business conditions. A word of caution in these combination environments,

TRADE-OFFS BETWEEN EFFICIENCY AND CREATIVITY

though: It is important to ensure not *every* analytic evolves into an R&D effort.

## *Example of the Balancing Act*

I once had an analyst who was asked to develop a new model to determine the probability that a customer would respond to an offer. Many probability-of-response models need to be updated frequently as marketing teams change the offers and as the competition adjust its offers as well. Therefore, this type of analytics usually turns into an assembly-line approach.

The modeler had access to a suite of over 1,200 data attributes. (*Data attributes* are raw data constructed into easy-to-use building blocks for most analytics.) The analyst decided to take the raw data and develop a fresh set of fifty new data attributes. Most of the new attributes were very similar to those already available in the 1,200-attribute suite. Unfortunately, the new data attributes possessed enough differences that, as part of the implementation of the new model, they needed to be coded into the system that would calculate the new probability of response. It seemed to me that the differences between the new and existing data attributes were minimal, but the analyst believed that they would add significant value to his solution. The problem was that coding the fifty new data attributes would take valuable resources and time, adding about eight to ten weeks to the process of implementation.

Before investing time and resources in coding the new

data attributes, I asked a different analyst to develop a version of the probability-of-response model with only the existing data attributes, and to compare the two analytics and measure the benefits of the new attributes. The results generated by both models were identical.

Don't misunderstand me—there are many times when new sources of data and new attributes *should* be explored and leveraged. The balancing act here involves figuring out how, and when, to allow analysts to explore new ideas.

In this case, the process of developing a response model was executed by the team that worked on the assembly-line analytic, whose main focus was to complete analytics as quickly as possible. And in order to continue to find improvements, we did agree to the have the assembly line team explore new sources of data and tools twice a year, though not as part of every analytic.

The hard trade-off with this balancing act is to weigh the value of R&D against that of canned analytics. While I have provided some guidelines, there are no hard-and-fast rules to finding the balance. You need to consider the choice between implementation speed, and the expense and effectiveness of the solution, for each business problem and analytical solution. Whether the team is approaching R&D through a Proof of Concept for every analytical they begin or adopting the more canned approach of customizing previously developed analytics for new clients, you need to make a conscious choice of how to effectively deploy your resources.

# CHAPTER 10

## ORGANIZE TO ENSURE CONTINUITY

ONE OF THE WORST-DESIGNED analytical teams I've seen involved about twenty analysts who were aligned to support one narcissistic modeler. The modeler at the center of this cult-like structure was the manager of the team and organized it to ensure that everyone's responsibilities were set up with one goal: to support his need to be the center of all activity.

He had developed a group in which he was the only person developing the majority of the analytics. I call such an organizational design an extreme version of a *spoke-and-hub system*—in this case, the manager was the hub, and the other team members the spokes who toiled to enable the hub.

The team had been organized in this manner for two reasons. One, as I have suggested, was to prop up the manager's immense ego. In his mind, no one was as smart, as talented, or had as much experience as he, and was therefore worthy enough to conduct the analytics. This came across in his treatment of the team and in his dealings with his internal and external customers.

He had also designed his team in a spoke and hub to ensure his job security, believing that, if he was the single point of focus, the company he worked for could never afford to let him go.

These are not the only reasons companies sometimes employ a spoke-and-hub design. Not having enough resources with sufficient domain knowledge will lead them to leverage it, too.

But by organizing in the spoke and hub, analytical teams often create a *huge* single point of failure. These organizations are vulnerable to massive delays if the critical analytical talent moves on. Moreover, the spoke-and-hub structure often creates an environment that does not fully leverage the talent *in* the spokes, thereby driving away talented resources.

Besides being inefficient, since all work has to thread through a single point, the spoke and hub often limits the opportunity to incorporate new ideas as well.

## Designing for Continuity of the Organization

Regardless of whether the organizational design is being leveraged, because of the ever-present issue of analyst attrition, management has to consider how to best ensure the *continuity* of the analytical team.

As I have pointed out, the demand for analytical talent is very high, always has been, and will continue to grow for the foreseeable future. Every analytical organization must develop mechanisms to work through the obstacles that result as analytical talent inevitably moves on. Consequently, it is essential that analytical organizations develop means through which analytical knowledge, business knowledge, and best practices are passed efficiently from subject-matter experts down to junior analysts.

In fact, without a strong knowledge-transfer process, analytic teams become more and more vulnerable to analyst attrition as strong analysts leave for the opportunities elsewhere to gain more knowledge. Furthermore, the teams are vulnerable to collapse or serious gridlock as critical subject-matter experts leave and the team needs to scramble to relearn critical knowledge or redevelop solutions they don't fully understand.

## Mechanisms for Knowledge Transfer

Mechanisms that help drive transfer of critical knowledge from experts to junior analysts include the following, which we will proceed to examine in greater detail individually (see Table 3):

### Table 3: Mechanisms for Knowledge Transfer

| | |
|---|---|
| *Organizational Design* | Place domain experts in key managerial positions and make them responsible for training junior analysts |

| *Documentation* | Documenting the process by which analytics are developed and validated, the sources of data, how to access them, data definitions, who the experts are on certain domains, and how to get in touch with them will ensure that knowledge can transfer quickly and efficiently across the organization. |
|---|---|
| *Peer Reviews* | Analysts put a lot of work into their analytics and can lose their objectivity. So establish peer reviews at critical points of the process. In addition to supporting knowledge transfer, peer reviews help produce better analytics by ensuring the analysts have not made any mistakes. Also a good way to introduce new ideas into the analytics. |
| *Analytical Council* | Similar to Peer Reviews, but usually more formal. |
| *Rotating R&D Projects* | Instead of having a set group of analysts support any R&D efforts, rotate the R&D responsibilities by project across the team. While helping knowledge transfer, this also helps bring in new ideas. |
| *Develop a maintenance team* | Maintenance teams are a good way to train junior analytic talent on the products, data, and analytical environment. |

Let's quickly explore each of these mechanisms.

## *Organizational Design*

In the ATOM method of analytics, a solid organization design is the key to having sufficient operational and domain knowledge. One option is to hire a few external operational experts and place them in essential management roles.

The hard part is finding individuals, with strong analytical experience and the right expertise, who want to manage analytical teams instead of conducting analytics. Many good analysts *like* doing the analytics and often choose to remain individual contributors instead of going into management roles.

Once an analytical leader locates their experts, they should place them strategically in the right managerial roles. In this way, the analytical leader can organize the junior and less-expensive analytical talent around these experts.

In their management roles, these experts can then help train the junior talent and gradually start to turn *them* into experts. Furthermore, as managers, these experts can more efficiently cover more analytical projects than they will if they execute the analytics themselves.

Organizing the analytical team around a few well-placed operational experts allows the organization to avoid the expense of having to hire analytical experts for every role. Moreover, by hiring on a few experts for a few critical management roles, the organization can avoid the vulnerability of single-threading through a single point of failure. (See Figure 1.)

## Figure 1: Example of How to Use Experts in Managerial Roles

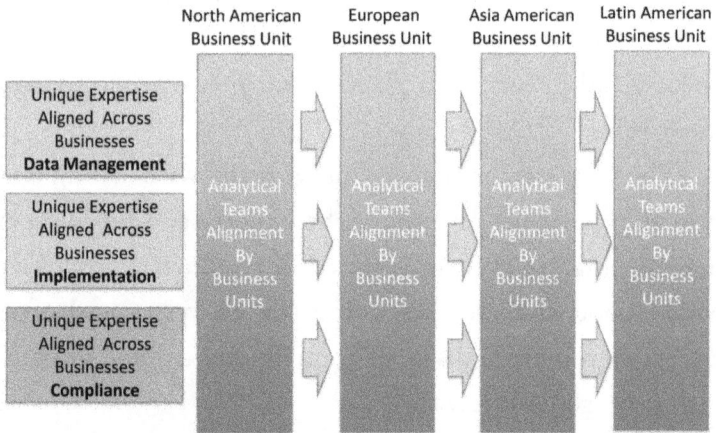

| | North American Business Unit | European Business Unit | Asia American Business Unit | Latin American Business Unit |
|---|---|---|---|---|
| **Unique Expertise Aligned Across Businesses Data Management** | | | | |
| **Unique Expertise Aligned Across Businesses Implementation** | Analytical Teams Alignment By Business Units | Analytical Teams Alignment By Business Units | Analytical Teams Alignment By Business Units | Analytical Teams Alignment By Business Units |
| **Unique Expertise Aligned Across Businesses Compliance** | | | | |

## Documentation

Complete and accurate documentation is a critical element in ensuring knowledge transfer. This includes documenting:

- The process by which all analytics are developed and validated. The analytical process should also describe where, in that development and validation process, reviews will take place, and who will be responsible for sign-offs.
- Each individual analytical solution must have documentation about how it was developed, the data use, and assumptions applied to the analytic. The documentation should always retain all validation and development results. Along

with the documentation, the analyst's develop-
ment-and-validation dataset should be archived,
along with the analyst's development code.

• Each source of data needs to be documented, including how to access the data, available time
frames, and any idiosyncrasies of, or gaps in,
the dataset.

• All data elements in each data source need to defined and well documented.

• Who the domain experts are, and how to contact
them, also needs to be documented.

## Peer Reviews

Peer reviews are one of the simplest mechanisms of
knowledge transfers yet also one of the most challenging
tools to implement in an analytical team. Many analysts
have a hard time accepting criticism with regard to how
they have conducted their analytic. I have often noticed
that analysts avoid peer reviews or cherry-pick the analysts
they invite to them. Conversely, many analysts have a
hard time deciding which issues are important enough to
discuss in a peer review, and the conversation bogs down
in minor details that slow the process of solution development.

Because, as I have said more than once, analysts put a
lot of work into their analytics, they can lose their objectivity. Establishing peer reviews at critical points of the
analytical process accomplishes many goals, including the

support of knowledge transfer and creation of another level of review to detect and correct mistakes before implementation. Finally, it is also a good way to introduce new ideas into the analytics. The key to peer reviews is establishing a cadence to when, how, and who will be part of these reviews.

## Incorporating Peer Reviews into the Analytical Process

All analytical teams need to document how they conduct their analytics. This should not be a static document and should evolve as the team evolves. The document that describes the analytical design process for the organization should clearly layout the points in the analytics when peer reviews need to be conducted. Also, the analytical development documentation should describe what will be covered in a peer review and who needs to attend. Lastly, there should be a sign-off process that examines the analytical solution prior to implementation. The sign-off process will examine the results of the analytics—did it follow the established development process, and, if not, why?—and the results and recommendation of the peer reviews

## Analytical Councils

Analytical councils are similar to peer reviews in that, at certain points in time, they evaluate the solutions being developed. Analytical councils are usually more formal and often consist of more senior analytic talent. Peer reviews include individuals from all levels of the organization.

### Rotating R&D Projects

Instead of having a set group of analysts support all R&D efforts, rotate the R&D responsibilities by project across various analysts on the team. Doing so allows junior and mid-level analysts to work with a variety of domain experts. While aiding in knowledge transfer, rotating talent in and out of the R&D process also helps bring in new ideas.

### Developing a maintenance team

As we discussed in Chapter 6, maintenance of analytical solutions is a critical but often-neglected element of analytics. Many analysts prefer to avoid this maintenance work. One solution, discussed in greater detail in Chapter 12, is to bring in junior talent to help process the maintenance work. Maintenance teams are a good entrance level role for junior analytic talent. The maintenance process provides junior analysts an opportunity to learn about the products, services, data, and analytical environment they will need to know for future roles. In this way, the maintenance process, instead of being a burden for the analytical team, becomes a mechanism of knowledge transfer and a pipeline of talent for the other analytical teams.

Moreover, as I mentioned in the discussion of talent in

Chapter 5, analytics requires an innate ability to understand the results of the data, and analytical organizations need a process to quickly assess how strong an analyst's skills are. The maintenance process provides the organization an opportunity to assess the junior talents' analytical capabilities with a minimum of risk and investment.

# CHAPTER 11

## THE GREAT DEBATE:
## "WHICH EXPERTISE?"

THERE HAS ALWAYS BEEN a debate in analytics over which analytical expertise teams should focus on. This question often comes up when new analytical executive leaders start their tenure, or as a business inevitably reorganizes. Furthermore, I have never encountered a shortage of opinion about which expertise is the most relevant to the types of solutions being developed.

My experience has been that, if you put three senior analysts in a room and ask them to create a list ranking the top three domains of expertise from 1 to 3, the end result will be six different number-one choices—and most opinions about which expertise is most critical are biased in favor of the part of the organization the individual supports.

At one of the banks I worked for, I was once asked to reorganize a number of disparate analytical teams into one global center for analytics. The team had to support analytical work across:

- Over a hundred countries
- Dozens of different products, such as mortgages, credit cards, commercial small business loans, checking accounts, etc.
- Dozens of different regulatory environments
- Different types of data with significant differences in data access, completeness, timeliness, and accuracy
- Hundreds of different systems environments
- Multiple business units that were mostly aligned by geography—each had its own president, whom I needed to keep happy

I spent the first month trying to understand the business needs. When I spoke to those business leaders, each firmly believed that the analytical talent needed to be aligned around *their* particular line of business. When I spoke to various senior analytical experts or support-function experts, such as Technology, all firmly believed that the structure should be aligned around *their* individual areas of expertise. Trying to organize these teams efficiently and keep everyone happy was impossible—and the most frustrating aspect of it was that each view I heard expressed had real merit. So in the end we did our best to design a hybrid structure that incorporated merits from a number of constituents.

First, we aligned the bulk of the analytical talent around each different business unit. We did so because I believed it was critical that the analytical teams developed solutions aligned to local business goals and current conditions. In addition, we consolidated specialists around certain critical areas of expertise. The key to the latter focus was that those specialists had domain knowledge needed across all business units. In this way, the domain experts became resources traveling across business units, specialists made available to all business-aligned analytical teams (see example in Figure 2).

## Figure 2: Hybrid Analytical Organizational Design

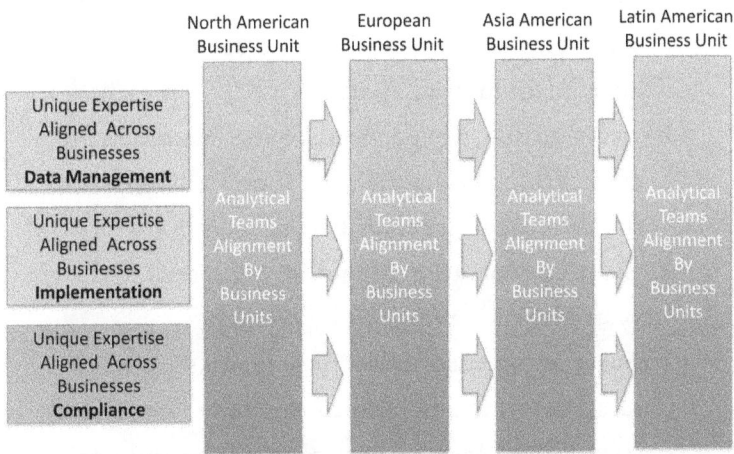

After spending a month socializing this organizational design and getting agreement from all the critical stakeholders, we rolled out the changes. Within months, these changes were received with positive feedback from both the internal customers and the analytical teams.

Several months later, I was on my way home one evening when I ran into the newly appointed head of Risk

Management for the bank. She stopped me on my way out to tell me she wanted to set up time with me the following week to talk about reorganizing the analytical teams around different types of products instead of business units.

## Organizing Analytical Expertise

There are many kinds of analytical expertise, including:

- Experts on specific analytical techniques, such as machine learning or non-linear optimization
- Experts on different products, such as mortgages, securities trading, cell phone services, insurance, or industrial analytics
- Experts on specific portions of the customer life-cycle, from the acquisition of new customers to the retention of existing ones
- Experts on various geographies, as access to data, systems, and laws vary by country
- Experts on various industries, such as insurance, retail sales, financial services, telecommunications health care, pharmaceuticals, or industrial analytics
- Experts specializing in the systems needed to *implement* the analytics—or various types of systems, data, and legal expertise

Most analytical organizations require a combination of these realms of expertise, but trying to design an organization across all of them is tricky.

In order to decide whether an analytical team may want to organize around a particular domain expertise, answers to the following questions will help:

*Internal or External Customers:* Are your analytics supporting internal or external customers?

*Broadly Used Expertise:* Is the domain knowledge required across most analytical solutions?

*Critical Mass:* Is there enough work, and do you have enough talent, to support organizing a team around a specific domain expertise?

Let's explore each of these questions.

### Internal vs. External Customers

Are your analytical customers *internal* or *external*?

*Internal Customers:* Aligning analytical talent in a manner that mirrors the businesses they are supporting usually works well. This is because understanding current business issues, objectives, and budget constraints usually results in better analytics.

*External Customers:* Aligning by product, specific industries, or customer contracts often work best. This is because understanding the customer's products, business model, issues, and constraints is usually critical to developing analytics that can be implemented efficiently.

### Broadly Used Expertise

Some domain knowledge is required across most solutions being developed. These varieties of domain expertise are good candidates for consolidation. After consolidating these experts into an accessible team, the critical knowledge can be more efficiently leveraged by all analytical teams.

Identifying which domain knowledge an analytical leader should consider consolidating specialists around is not, I must point out, always straightforward. Table 2-3 lists some of the characteristics of domain expertise that *should* be consolidated.

### *Table 4: Consolidating Domain Expertise*

| |
|---|
| Domain knowledge that is required by most solutions |
| Expertise that is hard to find and expensive to hire |
| Expertise that provides a competitive advantage and skills that other analysts need to be trained on |

### Critical Mass

The last characteristic that an analytical leader needs to think about when considering consolidating specialists is the concept of *critical mass*. It shows up in two ways.

First, critical mass requires that, for a given domain expertise, enough work exists to keep the specialists being consolidated busy.

Second, critical mass requires having enough analytical talent to create an effective analytical environment. Most successful analytics are collaborative in nature. So having enough analytical staff to create a collegial atmosphere in which ideas can be expressed, questions can be posed, and results can be debated is essential to the process of developing successful analytics.

# CHAPTER 12

## SIZE OF THE ANALYTICAL TEAM

I RECENTLY PARTICIPATED IN a conference of analytical leaders from the banking industry at which the breakout session on talent was standing room only. An industry leader in analytics recruiting talked about the results of a number of surveys that had recently been published by his firm and by a couple of large consulting firms. The underlying theme of these surveys was not a surprise, in that analytical companies expect to continue to recruit talent as demand for business analytics grow. What I found interesting was the *cause* of that growth. The surveys were consistent in revealing that the surveyed analytical leaders were working hard to fill roles in very specific domain requirements. The operational and domain knowledge driving the current demand for talent was focused on regulatory requirements and cyber security.

The current demand for analytical talent was not being driven, that is to say, by *revenue* growth but by *maintenance* functions. Whether prompted by regulators or by business needs, analytical leaders were building out their teams to sustain their current revenue models. So the demand for revenue is, for a short time, being overridden by a require-ment to maintain the quality of the current analytics solu-tions. As always, the pendulum will eventually swing back to driving revenue, which will then drive the demand for additional analytical talent that will focus on revenue gen-erating solutions. And in time these new solutions will again drive the demand for analytical talent to support the maintenance of these new solutions, and so on and so on.

As analytical leaders drive this ever-shifting pendulum, the key is for these leaders to develop processes that help them understand and assess demand for analytics in their organizations. This next section provides suggestions on how to develop those processes.

## Why Is the Rum Always Gone?

Companies that have analytical teams can quickly find themselves behaving like drunken pirates out on a binge in a Caribbean port of call. Like Captain Jack Sparrow in the *Pirates Of The Caribbean* films asking, after an evening of heavy drinking, "Why is the rum always gone?" many companies find themselves binging on their analytical tal-ent, only to ask, "Why is there never enough of this stuff?"

I once met with the head of analytics for IBM, which employs over a thousand data analysts. He told me, "IBM may have the largest analytics team in the world, but there are never enough people for the work." I have found this to be true of analytics teams of all shapes and sizes—there's always more work then people. Therefore, the key to managing a successful analytics team is to understand the work that is being requested, and then to organize and prioritize that work.

### Assess the Demand

The key to determining the right size of an analytical team is, first, to evaluate the demand for analytics. Regardless of their size, all analytical teams need a process that documents *all new requests for analytics*. This is essential, because once requests are documented and objectives fully understood, work can be prioritized and assigned to the right analysts. Analytical teams that accept work without proper documentation and fully defined goals, and from multiple customers, usually end up working in a chaotic atmosphere with delayed deliverables, bad analytics, and lots of rework.

Table 5 describes the purposes of processing analytical requests through a single point:

### Table 5: Reasons for Creating a Single Point of Entry for All Analytical Requests

| |
|---|
| To ensure all requests for analytics are well-documented and business goals fully understood |
| To use the completed documentation to gauge the scope of the analytical effort |

| To determine what type of analytical talent is required |
|---|
| To help prioritize the work based on business goals and size of the work effort |

I once inherited an analytical team that did not have an effective process for managing requests for analytics, which came from everywhere—dozens of sales teams, product development teams, product implementation teams, customer service inquiries, and various levels of management. These requests were dealt out to the next analyst in line as they were received, like cards at a poker table.

There was little documentation about which analytics were being requested, so the analysts had to spend a lot of their valuable time trying to grasp the nature of the deliverable. Often, moreover, the deliverables would evolve over time and result in massive workloads or dissatisfied customers. Furthermore, as these analytics were being assigned, there was often only limited understanding about the amount of work each analytic required. Consequently, deliverable dates were often assigned by the requester—and therefore frequently missed.

Even more problematic in this first-in, first-out method of assigning work, an analyst could be wasting time, achieving $50,000 worth of benefit while under-resourcing or ignoring a $1-million opportunity. With no tracking, prioritization was left to the analyst or was based on who was yelling the loudest.

## Assessing Capacity

Assessment of a team's current analytical capacity starts with all analysts documenting how they are spending their time. Preferably, each documents how much time they are spending on any specific request through software developed to track time. Currently, there are a number of time-tracking software types on the market, but I have also seen my fair share of spreadsheet-based tracking systems. Often at the end of the week the analysts are required to document how much time they have spent on each analytic, training, or other activity.

Once there is a reasonable history of what the team has been spending its time on, and how long various types of analytics take, the manager will have enough information to assess current capacity.

## Determining the Size of a Team

Once the team is tracking the demand for analytics and its current activities, all the manger needs to do is compare the demand to the current capacity. As Table 6 indicates, once armed with this information, it becomes a lot easier for the manager to:

### Table 6: Evaluating Demand vs. Capacity

| |
|---|
| Assess and justify the need for additional talent |
| Identify low-value activities that can be eliminated or reassigned to less costly resources |

Detect high-value activities that require additional resources

Identify bottlenecks where an investment of talent will improve speed to delivery and efficiency

Determine the type of talent that is most often required

## CHAPTER 13

### ANALYTICS RESOURCE FUNCTIONS

I HAVE TRIED TO make clear thus far that, since many types of analytical expertise exist, a good manager must orchestrate them effectively. As analytical teams grow, team work can be organized into five categories of responsibility in order to improve the efficiency of the workflow. These are:

- Analytical Consultants
- Deep Analytical Talent, including (a) analysts who work on one-and-done projects and (b) analysts who work on ongoing strategy development
- Analytical Maintenance
- Data Management
- Research and Development

We need to consider each of these categories of responsibility.

## *Analytical Consultants*

All analytics start with a customer, either internal or external. Understanding their business issues, products, business goals, and constraints is a requirement before embarking on any analytic.

One of the themes of this book, as I'm sure you have gathered by now, is that analytical talent often lacks the business expertise or communication skills required to fully understand a customer's needs or to translate analytical results into business requirements. Many analysts focus on details within the analytics that will only confuse most customers. Moreover, without the right operational and domain knowledge, the analysts often does not know the right questions to ask to get to the *heart* of those business needs. Without appropriate business experience, analytical teams can end up solving for the wrong business issue, or create a solution that cannot be used.

One way to bridge the gap between customer and hardcore analysts is to create a team of *analytical consultants*. Their role is to translate complex business conditions into an analytical design that is relevant to the business goals. They also translate analytical results into actionable business activities for the customer.

To bridge the gap between customer and analyst, competant analytical consultants need to possess the following qualities in order to produce effective and useful results (see Table 7):

# Table 7: Characteristics Of Analytical Consultants

**Prior Analytical Expertise:** These consultants have strong prior experience as analysts. They need to know how to conduct an analysis and have demonstrated that they can develop and implement successful analytics.

**Strong Communication Skills:** They also need to have strong communication skills and be as comfortable communicating with customers (internal and external) as they are with other analysts.

**Domain or Operational Knowledge:** They need to have the required domain knowledge as well. If they are going to talk to a customer about a fraud solution, for example, they need to have experience with fraud; or, if they are building a marketing solution for insurance, they need to understand the products and services being offered.

**Supports Sales Process:** Analytical consultants usually are a significant part of the sales process with either internal or external customers. They often have such a large impact on the sales process with external customers that it is not uncommon for their compensation to be aligned with the sales teams'.

# CHAPTER 14

## DEEP ANALYTICAL TALENT

DEEP ANALYTICAL TALENT INCLUDES those statisticians and mathematicians who enjoy working with data to uncover meaningful insights. Such talented people often have graduate degrees from universities worldwide. They are most comfortable discussing their results with other analysts. They serve as the engine of any analytical team, which occurs in two main forms, each best suited to differing analytical needs. Each form requires analytical talent with different sets of skills in order to be successful.

These two forms are:

- One-and-Done analytical projects
- Analytical strategy that requires continuous monitoring

### One-and-Done Analytical Projects

The first way to organize analytical talent is in support analytics that create solutions which, upon completion, are handed over to a customer (internal or external). The customer is often responsible for determining the best way to use a solution to drive desired business impacts, given their current business conditions (see Table 8).

## Table 8: Characteristics of One-and-Done Teams

*Math and Statistical Skills:* Analysts possess strong math, statistical, or other quantitative skills.

*Projects with Defined Starts and Ends:* The analytical work is usually assigned by project, with defined start and end periods.

*Operation or Domain Knowledge Not Required:* Neither skill is required if the team is supported by operational or domain experts such as analytical consultants.

*Inexpensive and Easier to Maintain:* This is the cheapest and easiest type of analytical team to assemble and maintain, since the team does not require domain expertise.

*Implementation Is the Customer's Responsibility:* Given current business conditions, the customer determines how to best implement the solution to drive desired business results.

*Customer Is Responsible for Maintenance:* The customer evaluates results and maintains the solution.

Analytical projects that fall under the One-and-Done category of analytics usually involve developing an analytical solution that gets handed off to a customer to maintain. The customer requests analytics for a particular business problem. The analytical team creates a solution to this problem based on real-time or historical data. Once the team has devised an effective solution, the customer examines it, and accepts and implements the solution in a manner that best meets their current business conditions, whatever they happen to be. After the solution is handed off to the customer, One-and-Done analytical teams move on to the next analytic.

The *dilemma* faced by this type of solution is that it flies in the face of real-world realities. *All* analytics are based on the assumption that the future will behave similarly to the data (historical or current) that are being used in the analytic. The problem is, both analytics and BI tools fatigue as business conditions change. In a One-and-Done analytic, the customer is responsible for monitoring and maintaining the analytic.

But, importantly, this maintenance process is often neglected—because the customer doesn't have either the resources or the systems that will be required to monitor their solutions, or the expertise required to maintain them.

This type of analytical team does, it cannot be denied, offer a number of positive benefits, which are outlined in Table 9.

## Table 9: Benefits of One-and-Done Teams

| |
|---|
| The analytics team is inexpensive to assemble and maintain. |
| This type of analytical team can support both internal and external customers. |
| This structure works well for research and product development. |
| Often, this is the type of analytical team organizations start with. All the organizations have to do is hire a few analysts, give them some data, and they are off and running. |

### Analytics That Require Continuous Monitoring

The second way to organize deep analytical talent is to support analytics that require continuous maintenance.

Some analytics are more prone to change due to the type of data that are being used, the industry they support, or the type of solutions being implemented.

For example, I once partnered with a small analytical company that had developed fraud-avoidance solutions for on-line merchants. These merchants wanted to identify fraudsters before they shipped the merchandise. Instead of selling the merchants a *point* solution, such as a software package, access to unique data, or an analytical model that predicted the likelihood of fraud, the company had its customers subscribe to a *service*, which included a software package, access to unique data, and customized analytics. However, because fraudsters were constantly evolving their methods of attack, with each subscription the merchants were *also* assigned analysts who created the initial analytics and, based on the results, *continuously refined them* over the term of the contract to optimize their effectiveness.

Table 10 describes the characteristics of these teams.

## Table 10: Characteristics of Continuous Support Analytics Teams

*Math and Statistical Skills:* The teams employ analysts with strong math, statistical, or other quantitative skills

*Analytics Are Continuously Being Refined:* The analytical work is usually assigned by type of solution, industry, or contract. Moreover, the solution results are continuously being evaluated to optimize the performance.

*Operation or Domain Knowledge Is Required:* Operational or domain expertise is required even if the team is supported by analytical consultants or other domain experts.

***Expensive and Difficult to Maintain:*** Hiring analysts with the right operational or domain knowledge can be a challenge and expensive. Also, the approach requires a strong training program to transfer domain knowledge to junior analysts.

***Implementation Is the Analytics Team's Responsibility:*** The analytics team is often responsible for determining how to best implement the solution to drive the desired business results.

***The Analytics Team Is Responsible for Maintenance:*** The analytics team is responsible for evaluating the results and optimizing the solution.

# CHAPTER 15

## ANALYTICAL MAINTENANCE TEAMS

ALL ANALYTICS FATIGUE OVER time. As a result, they need to be maintained. Many organizations give very little thought to how they'll do it.

Maintenance is required for two reasons:

• The world changes; therefore, analytics fatigue.
• Analysts work so hard on their analytics that they can lose their objectivity about how the analytics are performing.

Although it is counterintuitive to think so, even analytics that are continuously being updated with current results require *some* form of maintenance. Their underlying assumptions can change over time. These include regulatory changes, changes in customer preferences or goals, and industry or competitor changes not captured in the current results. Moreover, having someone else take a look at a team's analytics is a good way to bring in new ideas to keep the analytics competitive.

In some industries, and for some types of analytics, it is a regulatory requirement that the maintenance process be conducted by a team different from the one that developed the analytic. For other solutions, where poorly performing analytics could result in injury, or an error will result in significant financial losses, it is a very good idea to assign the maintenance process to teams other than the developers as well. This arm's-length maintenance process helps to ensure that the evaluation of the results is objective and unbiased.

As I have pointed out, one challenge maintenance teams face is that having a team that is only responsible for reviewing someone else's work is expensive. The challenge is that not many analysts want to spend all their time *reviewing* another analyst's work. This review is often boring and tedious, so that recruiting for the role can be a challenge.

## How to Set up Analytical Maintenance Teams

Maintenance teams have a set of responsibilities most seasoned analysts find boring, and they are expensive to keep up. Moreover, since they *are* expensive to keep up and do not generate results that, by themselves, drive business revenues, it is often difficult to get organizations to fund these teams.

One way to overcome the challenge of creating an arm's-length maintenance team is to set it up as an entry point into your analytics team. Doing so, and using it as a training ground for junior level talent, has a number of benefits.

- Newly hired junior analysts will be more willing to conduct maintenance analytics if they understand how they will be introduced to the data, products, and analytics environment. In this way, after 12 to 18 months of training, the maintenance team becomes a pipeline of talent for the other teams.
- Staffing with mostly junior talent helps to keep the cost of the maintenance team down.
- Furthermore, the dialog between the maintenance team and the development teams helps to transfer critical business knowledge and often leads to improved solutions.
- Also, for the hopefully rare occasions when demand and deliverables are critical, the maintenance team can support the overflow.

Obviously, a maintenance team with mostly junior talent needs to be managed by more mid-level analytical talent to ensure they are trained correctly, the work is being done correctly, and their observations are valid. Giving mid-level analysts an opportunity to manage a team of junior analysts is a good way to give promising analysts their first experience with managing and helps mitigate attrition.

Table 11 describes the features of these teams.

## Table 11: *Characteristics of Maintenance Teams*

*Math and Statistical Skills:* Junior analysts with strong math, statistical, or other quantitative skills need to be supported by more senior talent.

*All Analytics Are Periodically Reviewed:* The analytical work is usually assigned by type of solution. Some solutions fatigue more quickly, and those will often need more frequent review. Also, more impactful analytics should be reviewed more frequently.

*Operation or Domain Knowledge Is Not Required:* Operational or domain expertise is not required for the junior analysts. Depending on the size of the team, mid-level analysts will manage the team to ensure their observations are valid.

*Inexpensive and Easy To Maintain:* Hiring junior analysts, and using this team to create a pipeline of talent for the development teams, can be an inexpensive way to maintain the analytics.

Figure 3 shows that good analytics start with the customer, whose requirements are understood and translated by an analytical consultant with domain knowledge.

Depending on the type of solution required, those requirements are passed on either to a One-and-Done or to a Continuous analytics team. An arm's-length maintenance team periodically reviews the completed analytics to ensure performance and stability of the results.

The foundation of the four bases of analytics consists

of two additional teams. They are Research and Development and Data Management, which create a strong foundation for future analytics.

## Figure 3: The Four Bases of Analytics

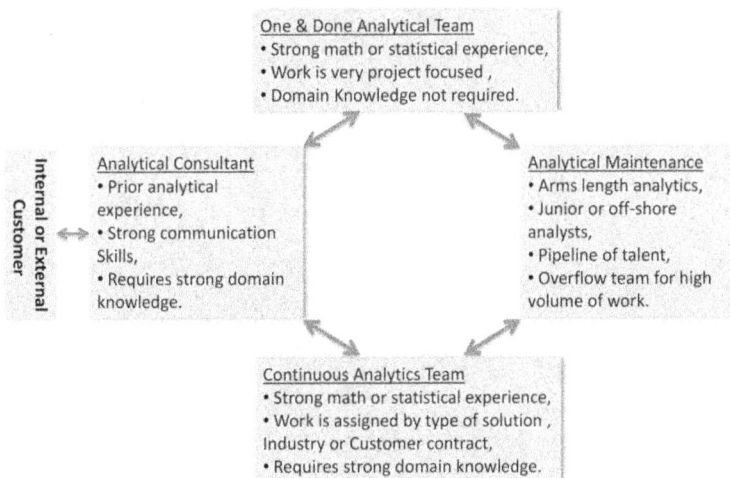

**One & Done Analytical Team**
- Strong math or statistical experience,
- Work is very project focused ,
- Domain Knowledge not required.

**Internal or External Customer**

**Analytical Consultant**
- Prior analytical experience,
- Strong communication Skills,
- Requires strong domain knowledge.

**Analytical Maintenance**
- Arms length analytics,
- Junior or off-shore analysts,
- Pipeline of talent,
- Overflow team for high volume of work.

**Continuous Analytics Team**
- Strong math or statistical experience,
- Work is assigned by type of solution , Industry or Customer contract,
- Requires strong domain knowledge.

# CHAPTER 16

## RESEARCH AND DEVELOPMENT TEAMS

ANALYTICAL RESEARCH AND DEVELOPMENT teams are responsible for investigating new analytical techniques and new sources of data, and conduct feasibility studies on new solutions. Many analysts find this work fascinating and enjoy working on these initiatives.

The challenge this type of work presents is that such initiatives often take a long time and use a lot of valuable analytical resources, as the analysts need to explore new data, tools, or solutions. Moreover, it is not uncommon that, while this work may find some incremental value, it is frequently insufficient to justify the resources needed to implement the proposed change. The rule of thumb is that, for every eight ideas explored by an R&D team, perhaps one results in a change that drives sufficient profit-and-loss impact to warrant the resources required for implementation.

Establishing an analytical R&D group can be a challenge, not only because it is an investment of resources, but because the other analytical teams can become envious of the time the team is given to explore new ideas. To avoid creating resentment that could encourage attrition, it is important to consider how to give the other analytical teams opportunities to work on new R&D concepts. What's more, if the R&D is a set group of analysts, introducing new concepts into the team can be a challenge, since these teams can become very insulated from the rest of the business.

## Rotate R&D Work

One method to avoid arousing any resentment and to bring new ideas to the R&D process is to rotate the analysts who work on R&D initiatives from across the other analytical teams. This method can be used as a reward for exceptional work. Additionally, rotating in new analysts helps introduce new ideas and keeps the R&D closer to the business and its goals. Furthermore, rotating the R&D analysts creates an additional mechanism to facilitate best-practices sharing and driving business knowledge across the organization.

## How to Manage the Costs of R&D

Here are three ways to help manage the expense of R&D efforts.

- Open Innovations: Open analytical contests are often established with a monetary incentive for the best solution. A company with a business problem usually initiates the contests, which challenge smart analysts outside (and sometimes inside) the business to solve the problem. Today, there are companies that help businesses sponsor open innovation contests. This type of research works well for a number of business issues. Those that contain proprietary information that the sponsor does want to publish are not, however, good candidates for an open innovation contest.

- Partner with Academia: Many universities have programs that partner with business to provide their students with real-world experience. Businesses enroll in the program, which usually requires some funding. The business provides real business problems, and the university organizes teams of students with a faculty advisor to work toward a solution. The company gets fairly inexpensive talent to work on a problem, introduces potentially new ideas into the analytic process, and creates a pipeline of potential future talent. The proprietary-information caveat mentioned above applies here, too.

- Partner With Other Companies: Partnering with other companies that have unique data, tools, or domain expertise that your organization does not have can be a useful way to determine whether a small company is a good investment or acquisition.

## Data Management Team

As I pointed out in the section on the four key elements of analytics, data management teams support the entire analyst infrastructure. They ensure the completeness, accuracy, and timeliness of the data used for analytics and for implementation of the solutions. They maintain those data definitions as well as how data and systems evolve over time. This helps ensure the reliability of the current solutions and makes development and implementation of future solution a lot easier.

A strong data management team also improves the productivity of all of the analysts and the solutions they create.

The team often provides options as well for implementations that would be onerous on the legacy production systems.

For example, I managed a team in one Latin American country in which the international analysts had developed a suite of models that, after eighteen months, had not been implemented into production. The implementation date kept getting pushed back, given its significant challenges.

The data management team found a way to implement a solution in which they retrieved data nightly from the bank's systems and scored the customers using this data and the new model. The scores would be sent back to the bank and uploaded every morning into their production systems. This solution resulted in $10 million in annual savings for the bank.

Together, the four bases of analytics, along with the two foundation elements, create a powerful environment for creating analytical solutions that drive business impacts (see Figure 4).

## Figure 4: The Four Bases of Analytics and the Two Foundation Elements

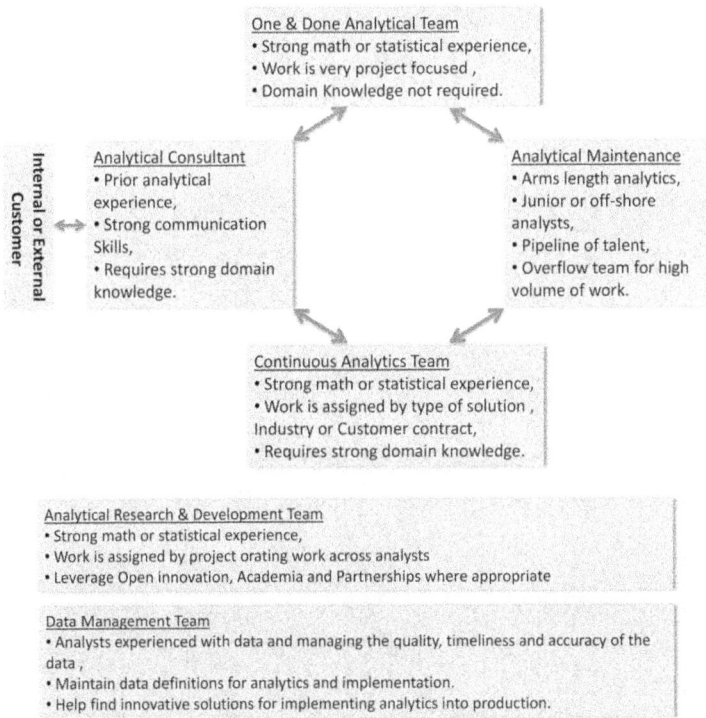

One & Done Analytical Team
• Strong math or statistical experience,
• Work is very project focused ,
• Domain Knowledge not required.

Internal or External Customer

Analytical Consultant
• Prior analytical experience,
• Strong communication Skills,
• Requires strong domain knowledge.

Analytical Maintenance
• Arms length analytics,
• Junior or off-shore analysts,
• Pipeline of talent,
• Overflow team for high volume of work.

Continuous Analytics Team
• Strong math or statistical experience,
• Work is assigned by type of solution , Industry or Customer contract,
• Requires strong domain knowledge.

Analytical Research & Development Team
• Strong math or statistical experience,
• Work is assigned by project orating work across analysts
• Leverage Open innovation, Academia and Partnerships where appropriate

Data Management Team
• Analysts experienced with data and managing the quality, timeliness and accuracy of the data ,
• Maintain data definitions for analytics and implementation.
• Help find innovative solutions for implementing analytics into production.

# SECTION 3

---

# THE FIVE STEPS
# TO GOOD
# BUSINESS ANALYTICS

# CHAPTER 17

## STEP ONE—DEFINING THE PROBLEM

MOST ANALYSTS START THEIR analytic by grabbing a large pile of data. They believe that there is some hidden code in those piles they have access to that, with just the right analytical technique, they will be able to crack. *Most analysts do not understand that the most successful analytics start, instead, with a well-defined business problem.*

Business problems usual come in the form of a question, such as:

- Who are my best or worse customers?
- What offers should I make them, and when should I make them?
- Why are my customers leaving?
- Which of our transactions are fraudulent?
- Who is influencing my customers?
- Where should I locate my next store?

All these questions reflect business problems across many industries. Without a well-defined problem, most analytics merely waste time and resources. Mining data in the hope of coming up with some hitherto-unobserved insight rarely creates any value.

Here's a good example: A large drugstore chain was looking to determine where to place its next emergency-care clinic. These clinics are expensive to set up and operate, and the client was looking for insights into locations that would drive foot traffic into the clinics.

Define the problem: *Where are the best places to open up an emergency-care clinic that will maximize revenue?*

The analyst got information from the drugstore chain about which clinic locations had the highest volume of sales and which had the lowest. The analytic teams then purchased, and evaluated, mountains of demographic data about these locations and consumers who lived in the vicinity of these locations.

The demographic data they purchased included, among other things:

- Population's age
- Median income
- Unemployment rates
- Real-estate prices
- Home-building permits
- Levels of education
- Recreational sports activities
- Purchase activities

But, despite using a variety of statistical approaches, they could not find a pattern that distinguished which locations would have a high volume of sales and which would not. So the analysts kept buying, and adding, more demographic data to the analytic in the hope of cracking the code. The results kept turning out the same. It puzzled the analysts that many of the unsuccessful locations possessed demographic characteristics similar to those of the successful locations.

Finally the analysts went back to the question again: *Where are the best places to open up an emergency-care clinic that will maximize revenue?*

When they thought about that question from a *business* perspective, they asked themselves, Who's *competing* with these emergency-care clinics?

It turned out that their biggest competitors were *hospital emergency rooms*. So the team went to the Internet and added one key data point to the analytic: *hospital emergency room wait times*, which are quite often published on the Internet. Once they had that information, all the pieces fell together. In combination with the demographic information, the analytic team discovered that the closer a location was to a hospital that had long emergency-room wait times, the higher the sales volume at the clinic.

Thus, the analytical team—using *both* the demographic data and the hospital waiting-time data—developed a model that could predict which potential emergency-care locations had the greatest probabilities of high sales volume.

Thus, without a well-defined business problem, analysts will try to fit the problem into the data they have access to. Yet in a successful analytic, the business problem needs to *define* what data are required for the analytic. Too many analytics have been developed that solve questions that have not actually been asked.

Still, having a well-defined business problem doesn't mean you're ready to start gathering data. You need one more critical ingredient—understanding how you are going to use the *results* of the analytic.

# CHAPTER 18

## STEP TWO—IDENTIFYING TOUCH POINTS

BUSINESS ANALYTICS, I REPEAT, are about people evaluating data to make better decisions. Yet in order to influence a business decision, the results of your analytic have to *precede* the moment at which people make their decision.

Say an analytical team develops a transactional fraud model that predicts high-risk wire transfers. No matter how efficient that model is, unless it runs *before the funds are released*, the model will not stop much fraud.

Similarly, offering a customer a mortgage *after* they've bought a house will not result in a lot of new mortgages. However, if you can develop an analytic that identifies consumers that are currently *in the market* for a new house or a new mortgage, and you can combine that with a tool that identifies which of these consumers will become *good* customers, you will have an analytic that can potentially drive revenue.

Moreover, once you have an analytic that identifies good potential mortgage customers, you need to consider the *points of influence* over those potential customers. These points might include mailing offers, Internet banner advertising, and teller notices at your local branches.

I call these points of influence *Touch Points*, and they exist everywhere in business and vary greatly depending on the business problem (see Table 12).

## Table 12: Examples Of Touch Points

| Business Problem | Potential Touch Points |
|---|---|
| Who are my best or worst customers? | Strategic planning and investment, annual budget process, customer service points, and online customer portals |
| What offers should I make them, and when should I make the offer? | Customer service points, online customer portals, mailings, and mass media |
| Why are my customers leaving? | Strategic planning and investment, annual budget process, customer service points, and online customer portals |
| Which transactions are fraudulent? | Customer points of service |
| Who is influencing my customers? | Online social media, mass media |
| Where should I place my next store? | Strategic planning and investment |
| Is this person who they say they are? | Customer service points, online customer portals |
| What products should I place on my shelves | Strategic planning and investment, annual budget process |

The next step for any analytic is to identify the Touch Points at which the results of your analytic can help people make better decisions. Knowing where the results of analytic will be *used* is the next step in designing any analytic.

To identify your Touch Points, you need to keep in mind the business problem the analytic is trying to solve, and to ask the following question: *Where will having the answer to that business problem help drive business results?*

Predicting short-term interest rates can help traders in the bond markets make real-time investment decisions. Moreover, the same tool that predicts short-term interest rates will help mortgage bankers predict the number of mortgages that they will need to process. Therefore, these managers can use the same tool used by a bond trader to assess staffing needs in mortgage-processing centers over the next several months.

A tool for predicting short-term interest rates may have two different uses, and each use may have its own unique Touch Point. A tool that predicts short-term interest rates can, for example, help bond traders make real-time investment decisions. In this case, bond traders need a tool that is updated constantly, taking into account new updated data.

A tool that predicts short-term interest rates will also help mortgage bankers, to take one example, predict the number of customers who will ask to refinance their current mortgage in order to take advantage of new lower interest rates. With this type of predictive tool, a mortgage banker can assess future staffing needs in mortgage-processing centers. Yet, unlike bond traders, mortgage bankers don't need the short-term interest rate model to run in hourly, or even daily. Staffing requirements—decisions to hire up or reduce staffing—are usually assessed, and changes made, every three to six months, not hourly, daily, or even weekly. Consequently, a model that predicts short-term interest rates can have very different Touch Points, with very different implementation needs.

# CHAPTER 19

## STEP THREE—UNDERSTANDING
## YOUR TOUCH POINTS

EVERY TOUCH POINT INTRODUCES constraints but offers opportunities for how to design your analytic. For example, consider the short-term interest rate example. Bond traders need real-time access to that prediction, and the frequent updates that take into account significant changes can mean the difference between making or losing money. But a quarterly update will be sufficient for managers running a mortgage-processing center, because no such center makes daily or hourly decisions about adding or reducing staff.

Some Touch Points are time sensitive and require real-time decision-making, such as whether an ATM transaction is fraudulent, or when a bank needs to know whether a person really is who they say they are before granting access to an online bank account.

In these real-time situations, it would not be helpful to design an analytic that requires data unavailable at the point of customer contact with the ATM or the online banking system. These transactions *could* be placed on hold and subsequently queued up so that the necessary data can be retrieved. But if you place on hold and queue up too many transactions, time starts ticking, and you can begin to lose your best customers. Alternatively, you can redesign the system to enable it to include valuable data in real time—but system changes that enable real-time access to data are often complex, expensive, and can take many months, even years, to complete in legacy systems.

When managers running a mortgage-processing center get a quarterly update, the analytic faces a lot fewer limitations on the kinds of data that can be used in the analytic due to constraints on data availability.

Let's consider three types of constraints on your Touch Points:

- The need for real-time decisions
- Regulatory and reputational risks
- Systemic or environmental constraints

## Why Not Real-Time Every Time

In today's world, with smart phones providing fingertip access to information, it seems odd to claim that not every decision *needs* access to real-time data. But in implementing analytics, a Touch Point that requires access to data that are updated in real-time can be very expensive, complex. . .and completely unnecessary.

To develop a model or test a theory in an analytical environment, the analyst gathers historical data to simulate making a decision in real-time. In such an environment, the analyst can, with a limited number of hurdles to overcome, bring together various data sources to simulate the decision that would have been made in the past had the solution been available.

For example, say a real estate agency, ABC Realtors, wants to predict which customers visiting its website are truly in the market to sell their home. ABC could gather information on who, in the recent past, listed their home with the agency. They could also, from MLS listing, identify those who listed their home with different agencies. And they could assemble data on who visited the agencies websites prior to those listing dates.

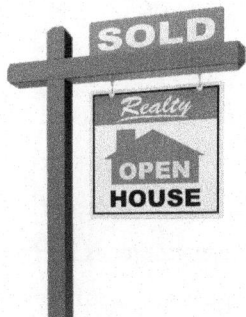

The analyst would probably see that those that listed with ABC, and many who did not list with ABC—or any agency—had visited the website.

So the analyst gathers demographic data about the customers who visited the website from the around the time they first visited it, and examines, in detail, what the visitor clicked on within the website.

Suppose, after some insightful analytics, the analyst figures out that the following combination of data will determine who is in the market to sell, and which of them are likely to list with ABC:

- A combination of items the customer clicks on in the website
- The value of their home
- The size of their mortgage
- Their net wealth
- How long they've lived at their current address
- Their credit-worthiness
- Their income

- The ages of their children

While it's not difficult to identify the combination of items the customer is clicking on in the company's website, gaining real-time access to access the *other* data items in the above list *while the customer is surfing the site* can be very complex, presents regulatory hurdles that need to be navigated, and gets costly.

What needs to be considered here is, *What is the most effective way to communicate with this potential customer?* Most people selling an asset as important as a home will not choose an agency to list with based only, or principally, on visiting a website. The process of finding a listing agent usually takes days, if not weeks.

Therefore, is the website really the best Touch Point for implementing a solution to your problem? The analysts also need to consider the complexity of the decision the customer is making, and the big-bothers factor. A full frontal assault on prospective customers on-line might turn them off because it's too complex to *absorb* in real time. Another red-flag issue we will explore in the Regulatory and Reputations Risks section is that, sometimes, customers can be very sensitive about companies having access to too much information about them on-line.

Perhaps a better Touch Point would be contact the customer via the mail—using the above model in a non-real-time process to send a prospective customer customized brochure information about listings that are comparable to their home, a view of recent listings and sales, and comments about the status of the market might be more effective.

The brochure solution could be implemented in batch, meaning *not* real-time. The information from the website, along with other important data, could be sent to data aggregators to be processed. The data from high-probability prospects could be sent to printers and mailed in days.

Moving that analytic solution into a production environment can also run into lots of constraints. Having your Touch Point access the same data the analyst brought together in a development environment can often create a significant systems burden. Moreover, interfacing with data sources that are external to your Touch Point, and requiring them in real time, create potentially unnecessary complexity and expense.

Table 13 asks a few questions to consider when thinking about using data in a real-time solution:

### Table 13: Considerations for Real-Time Data

| |
|---|
| Do the data have a significant impact on the solution? |
| Do the data change frequently enough to require accessing them in real time? |
| Does the decision being made with the analytical solution need to be made in real-time? |
| Is the real-time solution too complex for the customer to absorb in a short time frame? |
| Will the data being used in the real time solution create a problem with the customer? |

## Regulatory and Reputational Risk

Using data involves lots of *regulatory* risks. Having *access* to it doesn't always mean you can *use* it. This book will not review regulations, which vary by country and often, by state or province. There are usually ways to work within those regulations, but those paths depend on the merge of the data, the solution, and the regulations. My advice is, if you are not an expert in this area, find one.

The best way to manage regulatory risk is to engage experts early on, before resources are wasted developing solutions that cannot be implemented.

While regulatory issues are usually very black-and-white, *reputational risk* issues come in every shade of gray one can imagine. Also, to make matters more complex, the line between what is fine today and what will be fine tomorrow changes constantly as politics and people's opinions continue to evolve.

If your goal is not to offend anyone in acquiring data about them, or about what they do, in order to predict future behavior, you aren't going to wind up with a lot of data to analyze. So the goal around reputational risk is to make good business decisions. Therefore, before you start to use data for an analytic, you need to consider the following:

## 1. How Are the Data Being Used?

The kinds of data you use, and the kinds of solutions they're being used in, play a big role in reputational risk. For example, if customer data are being used to protect them from fraud, that is not usually a bad thing, except for the fraudsters—who actually *do* complain from time to time.

Consider the Edward Snowden example. People were upset that the NSA had access to their emails even though the NSA had acquired a court order to provide them. A lot of that concern was not about NSA using the information to stop terrorists, but about *what else* the NSA was going to do with those data.

On the other hand, Internet providers were giving a not-for-profit company the same data *without* a court order, because the only use of the data was to capture sexual predators.

One use of an individual's data that quickly gets you into a gray area involves a third party using an individual's data to make money. I'm not suggesting it can't be done, but there *are* issues to consider before implementing such solutions.

## 2. How Were the Data Obtained?

Was the person aware that their information would be sold or used by someone to predict their behavior, and did they give their consent? If the customer *has* provided such consent, activities such as selling or providing data to a third party to make money will not be an issue.

The question is, Who would *knowingly* provide their consent to sell their data and *not* be tricked into it because they checked off a box in four-point type?

There are lots of places today where people provide all sorts of personal information. Social media are a great example. They fall into a category I call "give to get," in which people are knowingly providing data about themselves because, somewhere, they see a benefit to themselves in doing so.

Here's an apt example. I was once on a plane, sitting

next to an executive from a large Internet company. We were discussing data privacy issues and got to the topic of give-to-get. He described a new application that his company was testing. The previous night, he had been having dinner with his wife and some friends and planned later to drive to the airport to pick up his daughter. Towards the end of the dinner, his phone alerted him that his daughter's plane was going to arrive late, and, based on traffic conditions to the airport, it told him when he would need to leave the restaurant in order to get there and the best route to take.

Like many other people, I have several apps on my phone each of which could provide a *portion* of that solution. While sitting at the dinner table, ignoring my companions (something my wife really hates), I would have had to go through all those apps to get that information— one for my daughter's flight details, another for traffic conditions, and perhaps a third for directions around the traffic. In the case I am describing, however, the executive had, within seconds, determined that he had enough time for dessert before heading out to the airport.

For his app to work, he needed to provide quite a bit of personal information, but he *got back* something he and many people find valuable. . .time to enjoy dessert. That's "give and get" in a nutshell.

### 3. *The Creepy Factor*

On February 12, 2012, Charles Duhigg wrote an article

on how Target identifies soon-to-be parents before their competition, so that they can turn them into loyal customers and sell them useful and not-so-useful items that many expectant parents buy. (My wife and I bought both kinds of items when our daughter was born. I'm still not sure what the Diaper Genie was supposed to do—it certainly did not make the dirty diapers disappear.)

The article centered on the actions of a smart young statistician, Andrew Pole. Target captures information about what its customers are buying. The company also buys demographic information about its customers. Pole took this historical purchase data, the demographic data, and the information from Target Baby registry to develop a model that—based on their current purchase behavior—predicted which Target customers were *pregnant*. More importantly, the model accurately estimated *due dates*, so that Target could use the predictive model to send these customer coupons timed to the stage of their pregnancy.

That model was a successful example of how to use data to drive business results—but it's also a good example of how to use data to make your customers uncomfortable.

Duhigg's piece provides an interesting anecdote about the pregnancy model. A year after the coupons were sent out, an irate man entered a Target near Minneapolis and, waving coupons, complained to the manager, "'My daughter got this in the mail! . . . She's still in high school, and you're sending her coupons for baby clothes and cribs? Are you trying to encourage her to get pregnant?'"

The manager, speechless, examined the mailer, which

had indeed been sent to the man's daughter, and indeed contained ads for maternity clothes and nursery furniture. He apologized and made a follow-up call to apologize again. The father awkwardly explained, "'I had a talk with my daughter. . . . It turns out there's been some activities in my house I haven't been completely aware of. She's due in August.'"

The Target Pregnancy Model is a great example of how, even if a company has access to data and stays within the privacy laws, its customers may be uncomfortable about *the use of* the data. Therefore, one of the factors to consider under the reputational-risk rubric is the *creepy factor*. If you predict something about a customer's behavior, are they going to be comfortable with what you know about them?

# CHAPTER 20

## STEP FOUR—SELECTING DATA

PLENTY OF REALLY SMART analysts develop terrible analytics because they use bad data. The term "bad data" doesn't refer only to quality issues like completeness, timeliness, and accuracy. It also includes more fundamental issues that can bias the results of an analytic. This chapter will review some of the bias issues that an analyst needs to consider in determining what data they will use for their analytics.

### Garbage in, Garbage out

Only after they're able to target analytics to a *defined business problem*, and understand—through the idea of Touch Points, how and where the results will be *applied*—can analysts profitably begin to consider the data that will best *fit* the analytics that have been defined.

When you consider what data to use for an analytic, a lot depends on what business problem is being solved and what is at stake. How complete, timely, and accurate any analytic needs to be will be determined by the nature of the problem it is trying to solve.

For example, consider an analytic that examines sensor data on rail-track conditions so that adjustments can be made to a locomotive to improve efficiency. In this case, access to real-time data is obviously required to drive the locomotive's efficiency. Also, given what is at stake if the analytic is incorrect, which could involve damage to an expensive piece of equipment or, however remote, the chance of creating a crash and endangering people's lives, the requirement for data cleanliness would be high.

On the other hand, an analytic that is trying to identify patterns of activities on a website—to identify a company's best customers, say, in order to mail them the next best offer—could leverage data that are days or weeks old. Moreover, given that these marketing analytics don't usually have enormous financial impacts, or life-or-death implications, the data that can be used in these analytics do not need to be absolutely pristine—that is, not always complete and entirely inaccurate.

As a result, regardless of the business problem being solved, analysts need to ask certain questions before pulling data (see Table 14).

### Table 14: Before Pulling Data

Is there sufficient data to solve for the business problem?
- Does the analytic need a dependent variable (the question being observed), and is there sufficient data to observe this output?
- Is there sufficient data for the independent variables (the input or causes variables) being used?

Does the analytic require historical data?
- Is the data's time frame relevant to the analytic?
  - ›Does the Observation or Performance Period of the analytic contain any systemic changes that can bias the results? (Note: The "Observation Period" is an interval of time during which you observe what a customer or sensor is doing—for example, a customer visiting a web site during a certain period of time. The "Performance Period" is an interval of time *after* the observation period, during which where you evaluate the outcome of what happened—for example, did the customer make a purchase sometime after visiting the website?)
- Does the sample need to take into account changes such as seasonal, economic, business, or regulatory changes?

Are the data available at the Touch Point, or do they have to be added for the analytic to perform appropriately?

What are the data-quality requirements for this analytic (including completeness, timeliness, and accuracy) that will solve *this business problem*?

There is no set formula for answering these data questions. Having the best data from timeliness, completeness, and accuracy perspectives is usually helpful; it is also expensive and not always easy to obtain.

Moreover, remember that not every analytic requires the cleanest, freshest, and most accurate data. A lot will depend on how cost and complexity compare to the impact the data will have on your analytic.

Let's explore each of these questions to get a better idea of what an analyst should consider.

## Question 1: Are There Sufficient Data to Solve for the Business Problem?

The important issue, when evaluating an analytic, is to determine whether it has enough data in it to ensure that the sample is large enough not to introduce any bias into the results. Entire university courses, I hasten to point out, are devoted to statistical sampling theory; my intention here is simply to mention a few key considerations to help avoid unintended bias.

**Segmentation Concerns:** Whether the analyst is building a report or a predictive model, or optimizing an existing strategy, it's essential to consider how the data are being segmented.

For example, suppose an analyst was trying to decide how to segment a report by geography. Should the analytic segment by all fifty states, or by several geographic regions? Part of the answer will depend on how the business is organized. Does the business have *sales* in all fifty states, or is it segmented into certain geographic regions?

Once the analysts understand the segmentation they are likely to use, they need to determine if they have enough relevant data for each segment. Suppose the report was looking at *average sales size* and all fifty states. In most states, the analysts discover, there were thousands of sales, but three of the states that had the biggest average only had a handful of sales. Because these three only had a few sales, their results for average sales size are vulnerable to being biased by a small number of larger sales.

The principle of having enough data by segment evaluated holds true for critical variables within the analytic such as the dependent variable and the output variable, and what the analytic is interested in observing, as well as the independent variables and the input or cause variables the analytic will use.

**Size and Degree of Accuracy:** There is also a relationship between sample size and *degree of accuracy* required for the analytic. As I have been at pains to remind you throughout, this book is not about learning statistics. In order to choose the correct sample size to achieve a given degree of accuracy, it is best to leverage the statistical talent on the team to answer those questions.

## Question 2: Does the Analytic Require Historical Data?

Many—but not all—analytics require historical data to help create and validate analytical assumptions. For those that *do* require historical data, ensuring that the time frame used does not introduce an unintended bias in the results is critical.

For example, developing a fraud model using five-year-old data is not usually going to be productive, since fraudsters are constantly changing their tactics. On the other hand, economists trying to predict short-term interest rates need to take into account economic cycles; therefore, they tend to analyze very long time frames of twenty-plus years.

When using historical data the following characteristics of the data should be understood:

- Stability of the data
- How long it takes to observe the outcome of the analysis
- Significant changes that may bias the analysis

**Stability Of The Data**: The key to understanding how far back in time your observation period needs to stretch lies in understanding the stability of data. The more stable the data, the more likely history is a reflection of the future. The more stable the data, the farther back in time the analyst could potentially go for data.

If the data are *not* stable—that is, if history is *not* a refection of what is happening today—then the analytics may require more recent data, more frequent updates, or both.

Fraud data is a terrific example of data that are not stable because the fraudsters continue to change and adapt their method of attack. Create a solution to stop them, and they will work to find another point of compromise to exploit. Therefore, fraud analytics need more recent data and are often updated to reflect the changing fraud landscapes.

One of my ex-colleagues now develops analytical solutions for companies that have large stores of data. Often he runs into clients who feel it necessary to include vast amounts of historical data in an analytical solution. It is as if companies with huge stores of data want to justify the expense of retaining those data by including all their data in every analytic. The problem is, as we saw with the fraud example above, not all analytics get better with more data. Businesses change, and so, frequently, do competition and the economy.

Therefore, instead of using years of historical data in every solution, one option is to develop an initial analytic solution with the most recent data. Then validate those initial analytics using the more historical data. If the analytic solution performs well on the most recent data as well as the more historical data then no need to change it the analytic. If the analytical solution works well for the most recent data but not well for the more historical data then it may make sense to understand what changed have happened in the past that are driving these different results. Once those differences have been isolated then question of using the more historical data in the analytic is based on the likelihood that these differences materialize again during the life of this new solution?

**How Long Does It Take to Observe the Outcome of the Analysis:** Also, if the outcome the analytic is trying to detect takes many months to observe, then the performance window needs to be of a sufficient length to allow for the analytic to observe the outcome it is evaluating. For example, if cell phone contracts are two years long and customers seldom purchase new equipment during the contract, then an analyst will need many months of data to determine the drivers of success with the introduction of a new cell phone.

Also, data are often impacted by seasonal cycles that need to be considered. Take the cell phone example above: If the majority of cell phone contracts expired around the holidays, then an analytic that used data only from July might not give the analysts accurate results.

*Significant Changes that May Bias the Analysis:* When using historical data, the analyst must consider any significant changes that have taken place during the observation and performance window.

Examples of significant changes during this window include the following:

- The company has changed its product offering
- The economy has gone into a recession
- The company's competition has just reduced their pricing on similar products

Significant changes impact the outcome of the analytic. So the analyst must consider which data period is most relevant to the analytic, given these changes, or how to account for them in the sample.

While no historical period is a perfect reflection of what the future may bring, all business analytics need to consider environmental changes that would bias any insights observed from a historical sample.

## Question 3: Are The Data Available At The Touch Point? Half A Loaf Of Bread Is Better Than No Loaf At All

At one bank I worked for, an analyst was asked to develop a new suite of models to determine the probability that a business would pay back a loan. The new model was being developed to support a large home improvement retailer who annually had hundred of thousands of businesses apply for new credit at the point of sale in stores all across the country. New models needed to be implemented in the Touch Point that allowed the bank to respond in less than eight seconds to credit applications at the store point of sale. The last thing the retailer wanted to do was create a long, cumbersome application process for customers waiting on a line with nail-guns and hammers.

The analyst decided to explore a new source of business data, so they purchased a large amount of the historical data for the new source of business data. Along with other data, the analyst developed a very strong suite of models that used the new data source. The problem was that the new source of data was not available on the point-of-sale system, so the models sat on the shelf for nearly two years, waiting for systems implementation.

I took over this analytic team after a bad regulatory audit, one of the findings of which was that the models being used by the home improvement retailer were old and required replacement. The regulators were particularly upset because the bank knew that the home improvement models had fatigued. Bank regulators don't have much of a sense of humor, and regardless of the excuse, they are not amused when a bank knows about an issue but does nothing about it.

When I asked the analytic team why the home-improvement models had not been replaced, I was told that new models had been developed but not implemented on the application system. The analytic team was very adamant that the delay had nothing to do with them.

When I investigated the cause of the delay, I uncovered the *new* source-of-business-data issue. The systems-development teams told me that providing access to the new source of business data on the application system was going to take significant resources and time. Moreover, the team was concerned about the response time. The company that stored and provided the new business data had no other customers with a response-time requirement, and could not guarantee the response time required by the bank's systems teams to support the home improvement retailer's point of sale.

When I went back to the analytics team to ask them if they had investigated the requirements and constraints of the home-improvement customers *before* they started to develop the model, they said they hadn't. They'd had one goal—to develop the most predictive model—and that was why they'd incorporated the new business data. Implementation issues were not their concern.

The problem was that, while this team had built a very strong predictive model using the new source of data, with just a *little* up-front investigation they would have discovered that implementing a solution with all that new data would be a real problem. The analysts could easily have updated the existing models that had been fatiguing with existing sources of data. While they would not have built the best models possible from an *analytical* perspective, they could have achieved a solution that was far better than what was currently in production. While this half-loaf solution wouldn't have been as good as the analytical solution with the new data, it would have been better than the fatigued models, avoided long implementation delays, and avoided angering the regulators (always a good idea).

Which was exactly what I had the team do—redevelop the models for the home improvement company using the data sources available in the application system. The solution without the new business data was far better than the existing models and was developed and implemented in less than six months.

So understanding where and how analytical solutions are going to be implemented, and the constraints in those Touch Points, is required before starting any analytic. And one of the first constraints that need to be explored is what data are available at that touch point, and will adding new data create implementation or execution issues.

## Question 4: What Are Data Quality Requirements for this Analytic Including, Completeness, Timeliness, and Accuracy of the Data for this Business Problem?

I once took a three-week management course with other capable managers from different parts of the multinational company I worked for. While I was working for the financial-service business unit, other students were involved in units that manufactured stuff.

One day I was sitting next to a fellow student, an engineer who, as he put it, "bent metal for a living." His unit manufactured jet engines, and he conducted analytics to

predict when critical parts of an engine would fatigue and need replacement. He used real-time performance data from the jet engines to anticipate replacement of critical parts before they malfunctioned and created more expensive damage. He explained that differences in flight conditions could require more frequent maintenance needs.

Having traveled frequently in my career, I really appreciated what this engineer was working on, and it was clear to me that his data requirements were different from those of the analytics I worked on. When I explained to him the types of analytics we did, and how often I had incomplete or stale data, he was shocked. I explained that, in credit analytics, I deal with large populations of consumers. While I credit-score every customer, I create credit policy at a portfolio level. For example, for a given portfolio, a bank may decide not to accept applications from populations of applicants with a probability of loss of 20 percent or higher. This is not a bad business decision, since it is hard for a bank to make money at a 20-plus-percent loss rate. But a population of applicants with a loss rate of 20 percent means that, for every one customer who does not intend to pay their bills, there are four in that population who have every intention of doing so.

The engineer was shocked, and said, "So to stop the one bad customer, I have to deny credit to four good ones?"

For some reason, I always appreciate the shocked look people give me when they start to understand credit analytics. I explained that I sure wished I could be more accurate, but the credit data didn't exist to allow for more accurate decisions about many populations. Therefore, it was not uncommon for my analytics to get it wrong four times out of every five. He said, "If my analytics got it wrong four times out of every five, planes would be falling out of the sky every day."

Different analytics thus have different data-quality requirements. Understanding them before the analyst starts pulling data can help avoid a lot of unnecessary work and expense. Understanding the consequences of errors in the analytics is the best way to determine data-quality needs. Those consequences include:

- Safety issues for customers or employees
- Impacts to equipment
- Large financial loss
- Regulatory or reputational risk.

Understanding your analytic's data-quality needs can help avoid a lot of costly errors and rework.

# CHAPTER 21

## STEP FIVE—ANALYZING THE DATA

NOW THAT THE ANALYST has defined the business problem, identified the Touch Points and their constraints, and determined which data will be used, he or she can finally begin analyzing that data.

These analytics can take a number of different forms—from reports that analyze the past, to models that predict the future, to analytics that optimize business decisions. Moreover, many different tools can be used to execute these analytics, from various statistical techniques to a variety of software programs.

The analysis needs to consider several critical issues regardless of the analytical technique used to evaluate data:

- The output of the analytic needs to be validated.
- The output of the analysts should be tested when possible.
- The output has to be consumable.

- Periodically, the results of the analysis should be used to refine the analytic.

Let's explore each of these issues:

## The Output of the Analytic Needs to Be Validated

Validating any analytic before using it to make business decisions is always a good idea. There are different ways to validate analytics.

One is to hold out a random sample of data from the development process. Once the analytic has been completed, the holdout data is sent through the analytic; the results from the held-out data should be similar to those from the development data.

Another validation method is to take a sample of data a *time period different from* that of the development data. Run this out-of-time sample through the just-developed analysis, and, again, the results should be similar to those from the development data.

## The Output of the Analysts Should De Tested When Possible

Testing the results means that, before the analytic is used to change a business process, the results get tried out on a smaller sample—a random sample of customers, or of a specific small geographic area—before a complete roll-out. Good testing usually provides additional data that can be used to refine the analytic and improve business results.

Many business managers get very excited by the results of an analytic and often decide to skip testing the results, because they're always under pressure to drive business results, and their analysts can show them validation results that indicate how the analytic will achieve those results.

The problem with this is that the real world is a very complex and dynamic place in which conditions rapidly change, as compared to the nice, neat, tidy one in which the analytic was developed. More than once in my career, I have seen managers convinced the new analytic will drive huge business benefits—only to find that they were absolutely wrong.

For example, take the wireless carrier that was convinced a new tool for identifying credit risk would result in over $100 million in new annual revenue. They rolled out the tool to all store dealership locations just before the busiest time of year—their Christmas holidays. That holiday season, they were very excited about the tool and used the new solution to open up a lot of new wireless accounts.

The next spring, they started to notice an increase in customers not paying their bills. The company saw an increase in the non-payment rates and focused their concerns on the new tool, blaming the vendor of the new tools for a bad solution.

After investigating, it was clear that a lot of changes had taken place in the prior year's holiday season that were *not reflected* in data used to develop the new tool. For example, in addition to implementing the new tool, the wireless carrier had changed all of its *other* credit tools at the same time, creating a lot of unexpected complexity.

*Also* at the same time, the wireless business was going through a significant change in marketing by moving customers to more expensive handsets and data plans. Finally, while the carrier was loosening up its credit criteria to accept more customers, its major competition was tightening its credit criteria—thereby pushing many more high-risk customers over to the carrier using the new solution.

Had the wireless carrier tested the new tool in a few markets that first holiday season, the results of the test could have been used to adjust the tool and avoid a doubling of the carrier's bad debt.

### The Results of the Analysis Should Be Periodically Used to Refine the Analytic

In analytics, it is easy to get caught up in a build-it-then-forget-it frame of thinking. In business, the next problem or crisis that needs analytical support is always showing up. Without an established mechanism for validating and updating solutions that have been implemented, an organization is vulnerable to competition, losing customers, making bad decisions, wasting resources and opportunities, and flirting with reputational risk.

All analytics need to be adjusted and refined over time. I call this "maintenance"; others call it a "feedback loop," still others "refinement." Regardless of what it is called, the analytic needs to be validated periodically and, based on those results, updated. If the analytical team doesn't set aside resources and time to maintain their analytics, most likely some other business priority will push the maintenance process to the back of the work queue.

# CHAPTER 22

## THE FUTURE

I'D LIKE TO END this guide with a few closing thoughts about why analytics in the business world will migrate from a competitive advantage into a business.

In the past, many companies gathered and analyzed data to find ways to look for competitive advantage. They would use that data to find efficiencies in their existing business model, find new customers, or test new products, services, or markets.

But this model is evolving. While companies still use data and analytics to look for competitive advantages, they're *also* now looking at the mountains of data they have stored as an opportunity to create *new* revenue streams.

Recently, I met with executives from an international telecom company that had created a new business unit with the goal of monetizing the customer data the company stores. This company had data about its customers— the services they had purchase and subscribed to—and tracked many of the activities their customers engaged in with their phones. I met with the company to explore ways of co-developing analytical solutions that we could bring to market.

During that ideation meeting, I suggested an analytical solution that would help the company reduce fraud losses on the phone services they sell. The answer the president of the business unit provided was revealing. He said that, while the idea of using their data to reduce fraud losses had value, his responsibility was not finding ways to reduce his company's fraud losses. It was to find new ways to use the data his company stored on its customers to create new revenue streams.

Today, hundreds of small to large companies are engaged in the very same activity. Large industrial firms that sell wind turbines are also selling analytics as a service that optimizes wind turbine efficiency. Small start-ups are finding new ways to evaluate email, prescription, or social media data to help pharmaceutical companies determine which physicians have the greatest influence on patient-treatment options. Companies are using their ever-increasing mountains of data to create new streams of revenue.

Analytics is evolving from being a tool to help a business find competitive advantages to becoming a business in itself. This is how analytics is changing the business landscape.

Let me provide another example of this change from a tool to a business. I met with a company that provided software services to automotive insurance companies.

This company's software helps create efficiencies in the underwriting of new customers, but a lot of its revenue was based on creating efficiencies in the disposition of auto-collision claims. It had grown very quickly in the previous few years and was very successful. Yet its executives were concerned about their future. The number of auto collisions has been dropping as automobiles have gotten safer with new technologies to help avoid collisions, and traffic regulations have gotten tougher.

Moreover, these executives were concerned that the decrease in collisions would only *accelerate* as the automotive companies brought more anti-collision technologies to market. So one executive was tasked to create new revenue streams using the data they had about consumers who applied for auto insurance or who'd had a fender bender. This company, which had successfully sold software, was now investing time and resources in a new business model that would develop analytical solutions to help other businesses sell more stuff or become more efficient. When I asked this executive why he thought his company could be successful selling analytical solutions, his answer was simple: "I'm already doing it. I'm just looking to expand what I'm doing."

As more companies create new sources or revenue using analytics or enhance their existing business models with analytics, I predict the following:

- Competition will drive more companies to use analytics to enhance their current business models or attempt to develop new revenue streams.

- Analytical companies will find out the hard way that they need to invest in the robust maintenance of their analytics solutions. This will occur as their analytical solutions fatigue and companies lose their competitive edge, businesses change vendors to move to better-performing solutions, or customers take legal action against their vendors for malpractice as fatiguing solutions create unexpected impacts.
- The demand for analytical talent will only become more severe, and analytical teams will have a hard time filling roles.

All of these issues can be avoided if, during this rush to develop solutions, the analytics leader takes the time to set up an analytics team for continued success. I've tried here to provide a good summary of the practices that will help create *successful* analytics.

www.ingramcontent.com/pod-product-compliance
Lightning Source LLC
Chambersburg PA
CBHW031936190326
41519CB00007B/554